Naturally SWEET

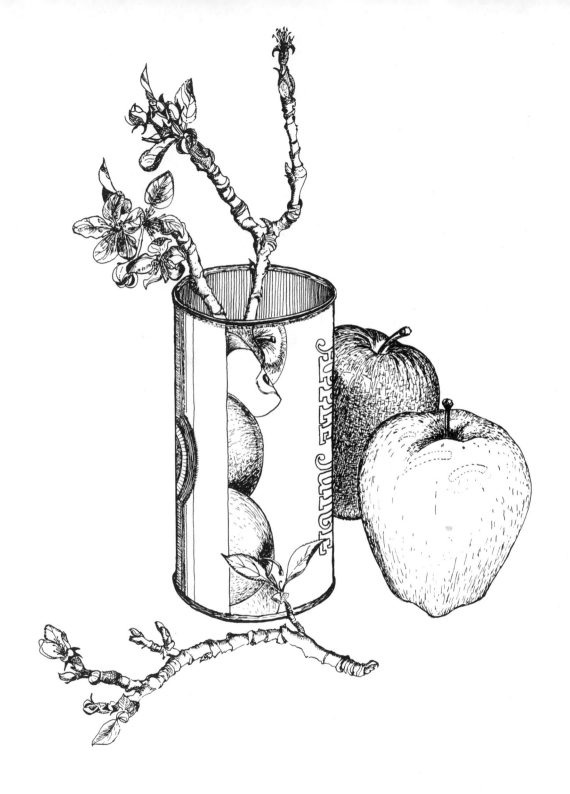

Naturally SWEET

Desserts Sweetened with Fruit

by

FRAN RABOFF
and LYNN BASSLER

Illustrated by Lynn Bassler

 THE CROSSING PRESS, FREEDOM, CA 95019

Edited by Andrea Chesman
Design by Ann Aspell and AnneMarie Arnold
Cover photo by Amy Sibiga

ISBN 0-89594-619-X

To the Walkers, the Allens, and the Basslers, all.

To Marjorie Simon and Julia Hess, who ignited a spark, and to Albert Raboff, who nurtured it.

Both authors are grateful to the many friends whose enthusiasm helped bring this book to fruition.

Contents

The Virtues of Naturally Sweet Desserts

& Some Baking Tips

One warm afternoon, about 9 years ago, Bob Bassler, Lynn's husband, appeared on the patio with a pitcher of iced tea sweetened with frozen apple juice concentrate – "tea juice," he called it. We all agreed it tasted delicious and marveled that its sweetness was accomplished without any sugar. While enjoying a second glass of Bob's special tea, we began to discuss the possibility of making desserts with apple juice concentrate as an alternative to sugar. We decided to test the idea right away.

Research proved that along with its sweetness, apple juice concentrate is packed with vitamins and minerals while having only half as many calories as an equal amount of honey. Inspired by the obvious benefits of consuming desserts made with a sweetener that is also a quality food, we began to experiment.

We weren't the first dessert makers to come up with the idea of using apple juice concentrate instead of sugar; many diet cookbooks have explored alternatives to sugar. But we often find diet desserts unsatisfying. Usually the recipes are disappointing – tasteless, heavy desserts, lacking in eye appeal.

This is not a diet book, though our desserts are generally lower in calories and fats than most traditional desserts. What we have created here are desserts that taste wonderful; that satisfy our aesthetic standards in texture, appearance, and style; and that offer real food value. We aren't calorie counters, but we do want our calories to count.

We accomplish this by sweetening our desserts with juice concentrate and with fresh and dried fruits. Thus our desserts contain vitamins, minerals, and fiber, rather than the empty calories of sugar. As for flavor, we think our virtuous desserts are superior to traditional sugar-ladened desserts. What we taste in a virtuous dessert are the sweet flavors of fruits and spices and the subtle

3

way the various ingredients interact. We think you will appreciate what a difference a naturally sweetened dessert can make.

Most of the recipes use unbleached all-purpose flour, but many have the option of using all or part whole wheat flour. Whole wheat flour contains the germ and bran of the wheat, which adds food value and fiber. A dessert made exclusively with whole wheat may be more healthful; but, we feel, such desserts are not sufficiently light and tender. Cakes become as firm as breads, crusts become dense and tough, and cookies seem crackerlike. Our compromise is to list our preference in each recipe, but to suggest an option where possible for a blend of whole wheat and unbleached flours.

As for the use of butter, margarine, and oil in virtuous desserts, we have taken a moderate approach. Eliminate the fat from desserts and the texture becomes unpleasantly dry and compact. We discovered, on the other hand, that the fat could be reduced in most recipes without making a noticeable difference. We were looking for a balance that would please and satisfy our craving for sweet-tasting desserts, without compromising our desire to eat healthfully. In most cases, we let you choose whether to use butter or margarine. And vegetable oil is specified only where it won't affect the texture.

So what is a virtuous dessert? It's a dessert for health-conscious people who want to get value from all the foods they eat. It's a dessert made with the natural sweet flavor of fruit and fruit juice, packed with vitamins and minerals and fiber, and low in fat. It's a dessert that tastes wonderful and has a satisfying texture, and that looks beautiful and appealing. And best of all, it is one that invigorates and provides nourishment for the body and soul.

A Word About the Ingredients

Like most desserts, our virtuous ones contain fruit, flour, eggs (sometimes), butter or margarine (as little as possible), nuts, and flavorings. Unlike most desserts, ours don't contain any sugar. So before we get started with

Apple Juice Concentrate
Compared to Sugar and Honey

	Juice (1 cup)	Sugar (1 cup)	Honey (1 cup)
Calories	448	770	1081
Protein	1.05 g	0 g	1.0 g
Carbohydrates	113.5 g	200 g	279 g
Calcium	56.7 mg	0 mg	17 mg
Phosphorus	86.2 mg	0 mg	20 mg
Iron	5.67 mg	.2 mg	1.7 mg
Sodium	10.5 mg	2 mg	17 mg
Potassium	963 mg	6 mg	173 mg
Thiamine (B1)	.063 mg	0 mg	.02 mg
Riboflavin (B2)	1.47 mg	0 mg	.14 mg
Niacin	.84 mg	0 mg	1.0 mg
Ascorbic acid (C)	8.4 mg	0 mg	3 mg

Source for figures in column 1: Matt Ivary, consultant. Source for figures in columns 2 and 3: *Nutritive Values of American Foods*, USDA Handbook No. 456, 1975.

the recipes, we thought it would be helpful to provide some tips about using apple juice concentrate and dried fruits as sweeteners, as well as provide some general tips concerning the use of the more familiar ingredients.

The Virtues of Frozen Apple Juice Concentrate

Frozen apple juice concentrate, available in most any supermarket right next to the frozen orange juice concentrate, is our sweetener of choice. It adds sweetness to a dessert as sugar does, while adding vitamins and minerals and fewer calories. Sometimes we use frozen orange juice concentrate instead of apple, but this adds flavor as well as sweetness.

Frozen apple juice concentrate is made by pressing

the juice from ripe apples and removing much of the water content through evaporation. The result is a clear, amber concentrate that will keep in your freezer or refrigerator.

What we do is keep a can of thawed concentrate in the refrigerator in a jar with a tight-fitting lid. This way it is ready to be measured by the spoonful or cupful into a recipe as needed. Kept tightly capped, it will retain its quality for several weeks in the refrigerator.

If you are using frozen (unthawed) juice concentrate, stir the frozen slush with a table knife for a few minutes to bring it to a more liquefied state. Then it will be easy to spoon out.

To properly combine the juice concentrate with ingredients such as butter or margarine, eggs, or milk, the juice concentrate should be at room temperature. You can warm it in a heatproof cup by placing it in a microwave or by placing it in a warm water bath and stirring until it no longer feels cold.

In recent years, there has been concern about chemical and pesticide residues in apple products. Our research indicates that several brands of apple juice test out as having acceptable levels of chemical residues, with more manufacturers planning to rely on chemical-free apples in the future. If you have questions about the purity of the juice concentrate you buy, we suggest you consult *Consumers Reports* or write to the manufacturer directly.

The Virtues of the Date

Many desserts cannot be sweetened solely with frozen apple juice concentrate because it contributes too much liquid. In such cases, we puree dates with the frozen apple juice concentrate, which thickens the concentrate and adds additional sweetness. When we puree dates with a little butter and apple juice concentrate, we make a thick paste that can replace the creamed butter and sugar in a cookie or cake recipe.

The date is a fresh fruit with properties like a dried fruit. Its water content is very low and its flavor is intensely sweet. There is little if any of the aroma and perfume we expect from fresh fruits. Dates contain about 21 calories each. They are high in fiber and low in sodium. They are also a rich source of potassium and iron.

You'll find dates in most supermarkets (look in the produce section or in the dried fruit section) and natural food stores year-round. A supply of dates will keep indefinitely in the freezer and for a very long time in the refrigerator. Occasionally very soft dates will ferment if left unrefrigerated. The appearance of sugar crystals, called sugaring up, is caused by loss of moisture and in no way will affect the edibility or the flavor of the date. Either wipe the dates off with a damp cloth, or place them on a cookie sheet, cover them with a damp cloth, and place them in a warm oven for a few minutes, until the skins reabsorb the crystallized date sugar.

There are no special tips for using dates. There is no need to wash them before preparing. Most packers automatically pit them before they are packaged. We find that snipping dates with a pair of kitchen scissors is an effective way to chop them. Also, because dates are irregular in shape and consistency, we prefer to measure them by weight rather than volume. If you do not have a scale, make sure your dates are well packed into the measuring cup. We have given both weight and volume in our recipes.

At many health food stores, you will have a variety of dates to choose from. The Deglet-Noor date is considered good for cooking. The Med-Jool is a larger, sweeter, moister date. It is also suitable for baking, but, because of its higher cost, it is most often eaten out of hand.

If you can't find a local source for dates, you can order them through the mail. Ninety-eight percent of the dates in this country come from the Coachella Valley, a semi-arid region in the southeastern corner of California. A reliable mail order source is the Valerie Jean Date Shop, P.O. Box 786, Thermal, CA 92274 (call 800-522-7799 for orders from within California; 800-828-5657 for orders outside of California). Valerie Jean produces Date Crunchies, which are dates already pitted and diced so they can be easily measured for baking. You can also order dates from Sun-Date, Inc.,

85-215 Avenue 50, Coachella, CA 92236; and Shield's Date Gardens, 80-225 Highway 111, Indio, CA 92201.

Dried Fruits

We use dried apricots, dried figs, and raisins in many of our recipes. Dried fruits add a lot of sweetness and flavor, as well as fiber, vitamins, and minerals. For the recipes in this book, it is important that the dried fruit you buy be strongly flavored and sweet. Taste before buying, if possible.

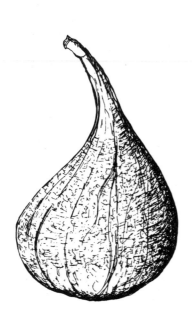

Many light-colored dried fruits (apricots, golden raisins) are treated with sulfur dioxide, which some people are allergic to, to prevent them from darkening. Untreated dried fruits are sold in natural food stores.

Purchase dried fruits when they come into season at the end of the summer harvest. Store them in a cool place or in the refrigerator for up to 2 months. In the freezer, dried fruits will keep indefinitely.

If your dried fruits are leathery and hard, they will not soften in baking. Place them in fruit juice for an hour to reconstitute, or plump them more quickly by cooking them in a little juice until the liquid is absorbed. Pat dry before using in a recipe.

Kitchen scissors are the ideal tool for chopping dried fruits. If your fruits are very sticky, dip the scissors in hot water before cutting or freeze the fruit for several hours.

Egg Whites

We use egg whites as a leavening in some recipes and to provide the light texture associated with meringues and chiffons. Egg whites have none of the fat and cholesterol associated with egg yolks, so we use them extensively.

Egg whites separate best when they are cold, but beat with more volume when they are at room temperature. So, when a recipe uses egg whites, separate the eggs first, while they are still cold, but beat them later. Watch that no yolk gets in with the whites, as its fat content will keep the whites from stiffening properly. To quickly bring egg whites to room temperature, place them in a bowl surrounded with hot water and stir until the whites are lukewarm.

All bowls, beaters, and utensils should be grease free. If you are in doubt about them being scrupulously clean, wipe them with a little vinegar.

Beat egg whites with an electric mixer, hand beater, or hand whisk. Start beating slowly. When the whites are foamy, add cream of tartar or salt, which act as stabilizers. Gradually increase the beating speed and continue to beat until the whites just begin to form shiny peaks that curl softly and remain in the wires of the beaters. Overbeaten egg whites will be dull, dry, and will not fold into a batter properly.

To fold beaten whites into a batter, gently stir and fold one-quarter of the whites into the batter to lighten it. Slide the whites into the bowl that holds the batter and fold in by cutting down through the mixture with a rubber spatula, scraping across the bottom of the bowl and bringing the spatula up, then smoothing it over the top of the mixture and bringing it back down. Repeat this circular motion and, at the same time, give the bowl a quarter-turn until almost all the whites are incorporated into the batter. Do not overmix or use a stirring motion.

When the whites are folded in, gently spoon the batter into a pan or bowl and bake or refrigerate immediately. Beaten egg whites will liquefy if allowed to stand, so it is not possible to prepare them ahead of time.

Flour

All-purpose flour is a blend of hard and soft wheat. It is balanced to provide good baking properties for most purposes. We specify unbleached all-purpose flour because it has not been treated with chemical bleaching agents.

Sifting is not necessary to measure out the amount of flour needed for the recipes here. A bag of commercial flour comes already sifted; however, the handling it takes to get it onto the market shelf causes it to compact. We suggest you fluff the flour right in the bag by stirring it. Then just spoon the flour out of the bag into a measuring cup, level off the excess with a knife without tapping or packing it, and then sift it into a mixing bowl.

Because the wheat germ in whole wheat flour is perishable, it is best to store whole wheat flour in airtight containers in the refrigerator or freezer. Allow the flour to come to room temperature after it has been measured and sifted.

Fresh Fruits

Simple fruit desserts and pies make good use of fresh fruits in season. Fruit desserts have the added virtue of packing in extra vitamins, minerals, and fiber, and many take very little time to prepare.

Use only the freshest and ripest fruit you can find. Fragrance is a good sign that a fruit has taste and quality. Many fruits that you buy in the supermarket are not yet ripe. To ripen fruit, store it at room temperature in a closed brown paper bag. To speed up ripening, place an apple or a ripe banana in the bag. Keep ripe fruit under refrigeration.

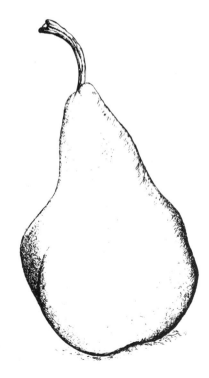

While supermarkets are doing a good job of importing fruits from all over the world to provide us with fresh produce year-round, we prefer to buy local fresh fruits at the peak of their seasons and freeze them for use throughout the year. When fresh fruit is called for in a recipe but not available, substitute unsweetened frozen or canned fruit.

Wash fruit just before using. Cut it in uniform sizes so it will cook evenly. Drain chopped fruits just before you use them in filled pastries so the pastry will be less apt to become soggy. To prevent sliced fruit from darkening, drop it in acidulated water made by combining 1 tablespoon lemon juice with 1 quart water.

We give the option of peeling or not peeling in many of our recipes. A lot of vitamins are lost when fruit is peeled and, besides, we like the additional texture the peels provide. But feel free to peel. To peel peaches easily, blanch them in boiling water for 30 seconds, then cool and peel.

Some Baking Tips

What is true for desserts in general is true for virtuous ones as well. Ovens should be preheated and temperatures should be accurate. Pan sizes should correspond to the recipe instructions. Substituting pans with different measurements makes baking times unpredictable. Fill pans to only two-thirds of their capacity to prevent batter from spilling over as it rises.

Many of the recipes call for lightly greased pans. To cut back on the amount of fat you use, spray your pans with a vegetable cooking spray instead of greasing with butter or margarine.

Cakes, Tortes, & Cheesecakes

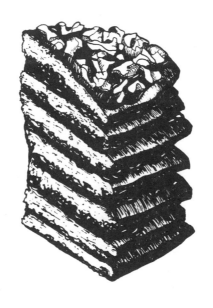

If you find yourself in the kitchen wishing there was a cake waiting on the counter, indulge the urge. Look up the recipe for a virtuous dessert such as Nutty Chocolate Brownie Cake or Currant Gingerbread. Both are healthful, hearty, full-flavored cakes made with nutritionally valuable sweeteners. Or make a cheesecake, which requires no special baking skills. The Tofu-Banana Cheesecake and the Cottage Cheesecake are both superbly delicious variations on the traditional cream cheese theme.

Of course, there are also special occasion cakes in this chapter, such as the Birthday Plum Cake, the many-layered Celebration Cake, and the Festive Fruitcake.

It is helpful to remember that baking times are approximate at best. Variations in the freshness of ingredients as well as oven size and temperature accuracy can have a significant influence on timing. About 5 minutes before you expect a cake to be done, check to determine its status by inserting a toothpick into the center. If it comes out dry and clean, the cake is done. Another test is to lightly touch the center of a cake with a fingertip. If the cake is done, the surface will spring back.

Once the baking is completed, place the cake on a wire rack to cool. Wait about 5 minutes, then release it from the sides of the pan with a knife. Unless the recipe states differently, remove a cake from its pan when it is completely cool.

Most cakes lose quality after a few days. Exceptions are the Festive Fruitcake and the Celebration Cake. Always refrigerate cakes that contain fruits or cream fillings and toppings until serving time. Wrap leftover cake and store it in the refrigerator or freezer. Cakes can be thawed overnight in the refrigerator. Virtuous dessert cakes contain no preservatives or white sugar (which acts as a preservative), so they must be carefully stored. Restore a freshly baked quality to the cake by warming it in a preheated 300° F. oven for 5 to 10 minutes.

Nutty Chocolate Brownie Cake

This recipe is adapted from an old Hershey's cocoa tin. It's part brownie, part cake, very moist, and full of nuts. Brownie Cake can be cut into small squares and served as a cookie.

2/3 cup unbleached all-
   purpose flour
3/4 teaspoon baking powder
1/4 teaspoon salt
1 cup chopped walnuts
1-1/2 ounces (1-1/2 squares)
   unsweetened baking
   chocolate
1/3 cup butter or margarine
1/2 cup (4 ounces) chopped
   dates, well packed
1/2 cup chopped raisins
2/3 cup frozen apple
   juice concentrate
2 eggs
1 teaspoon vanilla extract
1 teaspoon grated orange rind

Preheat the oven to 325° F. Grease an 8-inch by 8-inch baking pan.

In a large bowl, sift together the flour, baking powder, and salt. Stir in 3/4 cup of the walnuts, reserving 1/4 cup for the topping.

In a small saucepan, combine the chocolate, butter, dates, raisins, and apple juice concentrate. Stir over low heat until the butter and chocolate are melted. Remove from the heat and cool to lukewarm.

In a blender or food processor, puree the cooled chocolate mixture until smooth. Blend in the eggs, vanilla, and orange rind until just combined. Add the chocolate mixture to the dry ingredients, stirring just enough to blend. Spread in the greased pan. Sprinkle with the remaining 1/4 cup nuts. Bake for 20 to 25 minutes.

Cool the cake in its pan on a wire rack. While it is still warm, score the top into thirds in one direction and into quarters the other. Cut into 12 rectangles.

Yield: 12 servings

Currant Gingerbread

Currant gingerbread uses 2 kinds of ginger to guarantee a ginger bite. Dress it up for dessert with warm Applesweet Applesauce (page 187) or a whipped topping such as Light Milk Whip (page 210). It is delicious right out of the pan with a mug of hot apple cider.

2 cups unbleached all-
purpose flour (or use half
whole wheat pastry flour)
2-1/2 teaspoons ground ginger
1 teaspoon cinnamon
1/2 teaspoon ground cloves
1 teaspoon instant
coffee powder
2 teaspoons baking soda
3/4 cup dried currants
1-1/2 cups (12 ounces)
coarsely chopped dates,
well packed
3/4 cup frozen apple juice
concentrate, at room
temperature
1/3 cup butter or margarine,
at room temperature
1 teaspoon finely grated
fresh ginger root (or 1-1/2
to 2 teaspoons ground
ginger)
2 eggs
1 cup sour milk (add 2
teaspoons lemon juice to
1 cup milk and let stand
for 5 minutes) or buttermilk

Preheat the oven to 350° F. Lightly grease and flour an 11-inch by 7-inch baking pan.

Sift together the flour, ground ginger, cinnamon, cloves, coffee, and baking soda. Stir in the currants.

In a blender or food processor, puree the dates with the apple juice concentrate. Add the butter and fresh ginger root and mix well. Blend in the eggs until just combined. Transfer to a large bowl.

Add the dry ingredients to the date mixture alternately with the sour milk, stirring only enough to blend. Pour at once into the prepared pan. Bake for 20 to 25 minutes.

Cool the gingerbread in its pan on a wire rack before cutting into squares and removing from the pan.

Yield: Twenty-four 2-inch squares

Classic Carrot Cake

Our version of carrot cake is extra moist with a traditional cream cheese frosting.

1 cup unbleached all-
   purpose flour
3/4 cup whole wheat
   pastry flour
2 teaspoons baking soda
2 teaspoons cinnamon
2 teaspoons nutmeg
1 teaspoon allspice
1/4 teaspoon salt
1 cup golden raisins
3/4 cup frozen apple
   juice concentrate
3/4 cup vegetable oil
3 eggs
2 teaspoons vanilla extract
2 cups finely shredded raw
   carrots, packed
1 (8-ounce) can unsweetened
   crushed pineapple,
   well-drained
1/2 cup dark raisins, chopped
1/2 cup chopped walnuts
Cream Cheese Topping
   (page 212)

Preheat the oven to 350° F. Lightly grease two 8-inch round cake pans or one 13-inch by 9-inch baking pan.

Sift together the flours, baking soda, cinnamon, nutmeg, allspice, and salt.

In a small saucepan, combine the golden raisins and apple juice concentrate and simmer until the liquid is absorbed. Puree the mixture in a blender or food processor. Blend in the oil, eggs, and vanilla until just combined. Transfer to a bowl and stir in the carrots, pineapple, dark raisins, and walnuts.

Add the dry ingredients to the carrot mixture one-third at a time, stirring just enough to blend. Pour into the prepared pan(s). Bake for 40 to 45 minutes.

Cool the cake in its pan(s) on a wire rack. Remove from the round pans when cool and spread with frosting. Frost the 13-inch cake in the pan.

Yield: 10 servings

Spicy Applesauce-Oatmeal Cake

This cake is packed with the flavor of old-fashioned oatmeal cookies. We like to top it with a crunchy walnut-cream cheese frosting.

CAKE

1 cup whole wheat
    pastry flour
1/2 teaspoon baking soda
1/4 teaspoon salt
2/3 cup rolled oats
    (noninstant)
3/4 cup raisins
1/4 cup butter or margarine,
    at room temperature
2 eggs
3/4 cup unsweetened
    applesauce (see page 187)
1 teaspoon grated lemon rind
1-1/2 teaspoons cinnamon
1/2 teaspoon nutmeg
1/4 teaspoon ground cloves
3/4 cup frozen apple juice
    concentrate, at room
    temperature
1 teaspoon vanilla extract

WALNUT-CREAM
CHEESE FROSTING

3 ounces low-fat cream
    cheese, at room
    temperature
1/2 cup chopped walnuts
1/2 teaspoon vanilla extract
1-1/2 teaspoons frozen apple
    juice concentrate, at room
    temperature

Preheat the oven to 350° F. Lightly grease and flour a 9-inch by 9-inch baking pan.

In a bowl, sift together the flour, baking soda, and salt. Stir in the oats and raisins.

In another bowl, combine the butter and eggs, working them together with a fork. Add the applesauce, lemon rind, cinnamon, nutmeg, cloves, apple juice concentrate, and vanilla, stirring until well mixed. The mixture will be lumpy.

Add the dry ingredients to the applesauce mixture, stirring just enough to blend. Pour into the prepared pan. Bake for 45 to 50 minutes.

Cool the cake in its pan on a wire rack. Spread with frosting when cool. To make the frosting, beat the cream cheese until smooth. Stir in the walnuts and vanilla. Add enough apple juice concentrate to make a spreadable mixture.

Yield: 8 servings

Banana Maple Cake

The surprise in this cake is a crunchy peanut butter topping. The idea for this recipe came about as a result of a friend's habit of marathon banana and peanut butter snack sessions.

CAKE

2 cups unbleached all-
purpose flour (or 1-1/2 cups
all-purpose and 1/2 cup
whole wheat pastry flour)
2-1/2 teaspoons baking
powder
1/2 teaspoon baking soda
1/4 teaspoon salt
1-1/3 cups golden raisins
3/4 cup frozen apple
juice concentrate
1/2 cup butter or margarine,
at room temperature
1 cup mashed ripe bananas
2 eggs
1 teaspoon maple extract
1/2 cup sour milk (add
1/2 teaspoon lemon juice
to 1/2 cup milk and let
stand for 5 minutes) or
buttermilk

TOPPING

1 tablespoon nonfat dry
milk powder
1/8 teaspoon nutmeg
1/4 cup apple juice
1/2 cup unsweetened
crunchy peanut butter
1 or 2 bananas, sliced just
before serving

Preheat the oven to 325° F. Lightly grease and flour a 9-inch bundt or tube pan.

Sift together the flour, baking powder, baking soda, and salt.

In a small saucepan, combine the raisins and apple juice concentrate. Simmer until the raisins are slightly softened, about 2 minutes. Puree in a blender or food processor. Cool slightly, then blend in the butter, mashed bananas, eggs, and maple extract until just combined. Transfer to a large bowl.

Add the dry ingredients alternately with the sour milk to the banana mixture, stirring only enough to blend. Pour into the prepared pan. Bake for 45 to 50 minutes.

Cool the cake in its pan on a wire rack. Remove from the pan when cool.

To make the topping, combine the milk powder, nutmeg, and apple juice. Gradually add to the peanut butter, stirring until well blended. Just before serving, spread a thin layer of topping over the cake and decorate with slices of banana.

Yield: 10 to 12 servings

29 Palms Date Cake

This makes a wonderful grande finale for any festive occasion. Serve with Light Milk Whip (page 210) and a dash of freshly grated nutmeg.

1 cup (8 ounces) coarsely chopped dates
1/2 cup (4 ounces) finely chopped dates
1 cup orange juice
3/4 cup unbleached all-purpose flour
1 teaspoon baking powder
1 cup chopped pecans or other nuts
4 egg yolks, at room temperature
1 teaspoon vanilla extract
2 teaspoons grated orange rind
4 egg whites, at room temperature
1/4 teaspoon cream of tartar
1/4 teaspoon salt

Preheat the oven to 350° F. Lightly grease and flour an 8-inch springform or pan with a removable bottom.

In a saucepan, combine the 1 cup coarsely chopped dates with the orange juice. Simmer for 10 minutes or until most of the liquid is absorbed. Puree in a blender or food processor and set aside to cool.

Sift together the flour and baking powder. Stir in the pecans and the remaining 1/2 cup finely chopped dates.

In a mixing bowl, beat the egg yolks until thick and lemon-colored. Add the vanilla, orange rind, and cooled date mixture. Add the dry ingredients, stirring only enough to blend.

Beat the egg whites until foamy. Add the cream of tartar and salt and continue to beat until stiff but not dry. Stir one-quarter of the egg whites into the batter, then gently fold in the rest. Spoon the batter into the prepared pan. Bake for 30 to 35 minutes.

Cool the cake in its pan on a wire rack. Remove from the pan when cool.

Yield: 8 servings

Citrus-Glazed Prune Cake

Beneath a shiny tart glaze is a dark, moist cake. Its prune flavor is heightened by the aromatic flavors of lemon and orange.

CAKE

1-1/2 cups unbleached all-
    purpose flour
1 teaspoon baking powder
1/2 teaspoon baking soda
1/4 teaspoon salt
2 teaspoons cinnamon
1/2 teaspoon nutmeg
1/2 cup chopped nuts
1/2 cup raisins
1-1/2 cups chopped prunes,
    well packed
3/4 cup frozen apple
    juice concentrate
1 tablespoon lemon juice
1 tablespoon grated
    lemon rind
2 tablespoons orange juice
3/4 cup buttermilk
1/2 cup butter or margarine,
    at room temperature
2 eggs
1 teaspoon vanilla extract

GLAZE

6 tablespoons frozen apple
    juice concentrate
1/2 cup orange juice
1 tablespoon cornstarch
2 tablespoons lemon juice
2 teaspoons grated lemon rind
Pinch salt
1 tablespoon butter

Preheat the oven to 350° F. Lightly grease and flour two 8-inch round cake pans.

Sift together the flour, baking powder, baking soda, salt, cinnamon, and nutmeg. Stir in the nuts and raisins.

In a small saucepan, simmer the prunes, 3/4 cup apple juice concentrate, lemon juice, lemon rind, and orange juice for 8 to 10 minutes or until most of the liquid is absorbed. Puree in a blender or food processor, adding the buttermilk and butter. When smooth, add the eggs and vanilla. Continue to blend until just combined. Transfer to a large bowl.

Add the dry ingredients to the prune mixture, stirring only enough to combine. Spoon into the prepared pans. Bake for 25 to 30 minutes.

Cool the layers in their pans on wire racks. Remove from the pans when completely cool and set aside for glazing.

To make the glaze, combine the remaining 6 table-spoons apple juice concentrate and the 1/2 cup orange juice in a small saucepan. Bring to a boil. Stir in the cornstarch dissolved in the 2 tablespoons lemon juice; then stir in the lemon rind and salt. Continue to boil for 1 minute, stirring constantly. Remove from the heat and stir in the butter. Place one cake layer on a platter and spread with half of the glaze. Place the second layer on top and cover with the remaining glaze.

To store leftover cake in the refrigerator, insert a few toothpicks in the top of cake, then wrap. Only the unglazed layers can be frozen; glaze them when defrosted.

Yield: 10 servings

Zucchini Spice Cake

If zucchini has mercilessly multiplied in your garden, you'll welcome this recipe for spice cake. A moist, hearty cake, it needs no frosting. It's perfect for lunch boxes and afternoon snacks. Dress it up for dessert with Whipped Cheese Topping (page 211).

2 cups unbleached all-purpose flour (or use half whole wheat pastry flour)

1-1/2 teaspoons baking soda

1/2 teaspoon salt

1/2 teaspoon ground cloves

1/2 teaspoon allspice

1/4 teaspoon cinnamon

1/2 cup chopped walnuts

2/3 cup (5 ounces) chopped dates, well packed

1 cup frozen apple juice concentrate, at room temperature

1/2 cup butter or margarine, at room temperature

2 eggs

3 cups grated raw zucchini, lightly packed

Preheat the oven to 350° F. Lightly grease and flour a 13-inch by 9-inch baking pan or 9-inch bundt pan.

Sift together the flour, baking soda, salt, cloves, allspice, and cinnamon. Stir in the nuts.

In a blender or food processor, puree the dates with the apple juice concentrate and butter. Add the eggs and blend until just combined. Transfer the mixture to a bowl and stir in the zucchini.

Add the dry ingredients to the zucchini mixture, mixing only enough to blend. Spoon into the prepared pan. Bake for 35 to 40 minutes (50 to 55 minutes for the bundt pan).

Cool the cake in its pan on a wire rack. Remove from the bundt pan when cool. Serve without frosting or frost with Whipped Cheese Topping (page 211).

Yield: 10 to 12 servings

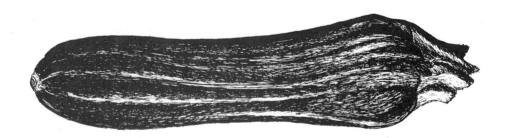

Birthday Plum Cake

A lovely single-layer cake that is split, layered with plum and cream cheese filling, and crowned with a broiled almond topping. A guest was so impressed by this cake that she commissioned three to be baked and secretly delivered to a surprise alfresco birthday party. Ever after it has been known as Birthday Plum Cake.

Halved and pitted fresh prune plums freeze well for up to 12 months.

CAKE

1/2 cup frozen apple
  juice concentrate
3/4 cup golden raisins
4 egg yolks, at
  room temperature
1 teaspoon grated
  lemon rind
1 teaspoon vanilla extract
1/2 cup unbleached all-
  purpose flour
1/2 cup whole wheat
  pastry flour
4 egg whites, at
  room temperature
1/4 teaspoon cream
  of tartar
1/4 teaspoon salt

Preheat the oven to 300° F. Lightly grease and flour an 8-inch round cake pan.

In a small saucepan, combine the apple juice concentrate and raisins. Simmer until the raisins are slightly softened, 2 to 3 minutes. Puree in a blender or food processor. Set aside to cool.

In a bowl, beat the egg yolks until thick and pale yellow in color. Add the lemon rind, vanilla, and cooled raisin puree. Stir in the flours until just combined.

Beat the egg whites until foamy. Add the cream of tartar and salt and continue to beat until stiff but not dry. Stir one-quarter of the egg whites into the flour mixture,

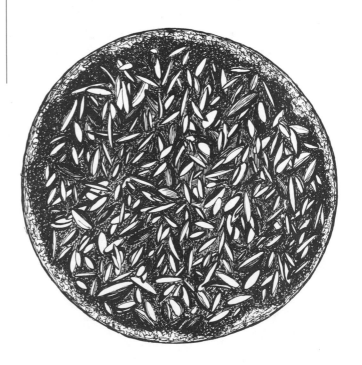

24

TOPPING

1/2 cup sliced almonds
3 tablespoons butter or
   margarine
2 tablespoons frozen apple
   juice concentrate
1 tablespoon nonfat dry
   milk powder
1/2 teaspoon vanilla extract

FILLING

6 prune plums, sliced
1 small pear, chopped
2 tablespoons apple
   juice concentrate
8 ounces low-fat cream
   cheese or ricotta cheese,
   at room temperature
1 teaspoon grated
   lemon rind
1/4 teaspoon lemon extract

then gently fold in the rest. Spoon the batter into the prepared pan. Bake for 30 minutes.

Cool the cake in its pan on a wire rack. Remove from the pan when cool.

To make the topping, combine the almonds, butter, apple juice concentrate, dry milk, and vanilla in a small saucepan. Cook over low heat until bubbly.

Split the cake horizontally. Place the top layer on a baking sheet cut side down and spread with topping. Slip under broiler for 3 to 4 minutes. When the topping bubbles, remove and cool until hardened.

To make the filling, heat the plums, chopped pear, and apple juice concentrate in a small saucepan. Simmer over low heat, stirring gently, until the fruit is barely tender. Place the mixture in a colander over a bowl. After draining, set the fruit aside, returning the juices to the saucepan. Boil until slightly thickened.

Beat the cream cheese with the lemon rind and lemon extract until fluffy. Fold in the cooked fruit, adding enough of the thickened juice to make the mixture spreadable. Cover the bottom half of the cake with filling. Gently lay the glazed layer over the filling to complete the cake. Refrigerate the cake until you are ready to serve it.

Yield: 6 to 8 servings

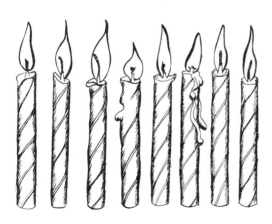

Festive Fruitcake

Typically, fruitcake is made well in advance of the holiday season so it can age. It is a test of willpower to see it "resting" in the back of the refrigerator. Although this fruitcake can be served after 2 days, it will continue to mellow and improve for up to 2 months if refrigerated. It is packed with dried fruits and nuts but is not overly sweet like the traditional cakes that are made with candied fruit.

2 cups quartered
    dried apricots
1 cup (8 ounces) whole pitted
    dates, well packed
1 cup golden raisins
1 tablespoon grated
    orange rind
3/4 cup frozen apple
    juice concentrate
1 cup unbleached all-
    purpose flour
1/2 teaspoon baking powder
3 eggs, lightly beaten
1/3 cup milk
1 teaspoon vanilla or
    brandy extract
1-1/4 cups whole almonds
1-1/4 cups walnut pieces

Cut pieces of brown paper bag or parchment paper to fit the bottom and sides of a 5-inch by 9-inch loaf pan. Lightly grease both sides of the paper and place in the greased pan. Preheat the oven to 300° F.

In a bowl, combine the apricots, dates, raisins, and orange rind. Heat the apple juice concentrate just to the boiling point and pour over the fruit, mixing until thoroughly coated. Set aside.

Sift together the flour and baking powder.

In another bowl, combine the eggs, milk, and vanilla. Stir into the fruits along with the flour mixture and nuts. Mix until thoroughly combined. Spoon the batter into the prepared pan, pressing the mixture into the corners. Bake for about 1-1/2 hours.

Cool on a wire rack before removing from the pan. Peel off the paper and wrap tightly. Chill for at least 2 days before slicing or keep up to 2 months under refrigeration.

Yield: 1 loaf

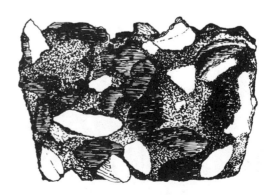

Peach Savarin

Our version of this French dessert is made with a light yeast dough, baked in a ring mold, then soaked while still warm with a spicy citrus syrup. The center is filled with sliced peaches or, to vary the filling, substitute 2 cups of unsweetened sliced pears. Serve with the Light Milk Whip (page 210). You will need to allow an hour for the cake dough to rise.

CAKE

1/4 cup lukewarm water
   (105° F. to 115° F.)
1 package dry yeast
   (1 tablespoon)
1-1/2 cups sifted unbleached
   all-purpose flour
1/4 teaspoon salt
2 eggs, slightly beaten
1/4 cup frozen apple
   juice concentrate, at
   room temperature
1/2 cup butter or
   margarine, at room
   temperature
1 teaspoon grated
   lemon rind

SYRUP

1 cup frozen apple
   juice concentrate
2 lemon slices
1 orange slice
1 cinnamon stick
2 cloves
1 teaspoon vanilla extract
1 teaspoon rum extract

FILLING

2 cups unsweetened
   peaches, peeled and sliced
   (fresh, canned, or frozen
   and defrosted)

Lightly grease a 9-inch ring mold.

To make the cake, place the water in a small bowl and sprinkle the yeast over it. Let stand for 5 minutes, then stir to dissolve.

In a mixing bowl, combine the flour and salt. Stir in the dissolved yeast, eggs, and apple juice concentrate. Beat until very smooth. Add the butter and lemon rind and continue to beat until the butter is well-blended into the batter.

Spoon the batter into the prepared mold. Cover with a towel and let rise in a warm place until the batter just fills the mold, about 1 hour.

Preheat the oven to 375° F. Bake the cake for 30 to 35 minutes.

Meanwhile, prepare the syrup. In a saucepan, heat the apple juice concentrate, lemon and orange slices, cinnamon stick, and cloves. Bring to a boil, then simmer, uncovered, for 10 minutes. Strain and add the vanilla and rum extracts.

Leave the savarin in the mold for 5 minutes. Then carefully turn it out of the mold onto a serving platter. Spoon the hot syrup over it. When it has cooled slightly, fill the center with the drained sliced peaches and serve.

Yield: 6 servings

Celebration Cake

If you've got a celebration coming up, this cake may be just perfect for the occasion. Seven cookie-like rounds are layered with fruit purees to make 24 striking servings. As a final touch, pass the Light Milk Whip (page 210).

Plan to make Celebration Cake well ahead of time to allow the flavor and texture to ripen. It should be allowed to age 6 to 7 days in the refrigerator, or 2 to 3 days in the freezer.

All the components of Celebration Cake can be prepared several days ahead. You will need to allow 1 hour for the dough to chill.

CAKE

4 cups unbleached all-
    purpose flour (or use half
    whole wheat pastry flour)
3 teaspoons baking powder
1/2 teaspoon salt
1/2 cup frozen apple
    juice concentrate
1 cup golden raisins
1 cup butter or margarine,
    at room temperature
3 eggs
1 teaspoon vanilla extract
2 teaspoons grated
    lemon rind

PRUNE FILLING

3-3/4 cups pitted prunes,
    well packed
1/4 cup frozen apple
    juice concentrate
Water
1 teaspoon grated
    lemon rind
1/2 teaspoon nutmeg

To make the cake layers, sift together the flour, baking powder, and salt. Set aside.

In a small saucepan, combine the apple juice concentrate and raisins. Simmer until the raisins are slightly softened, 2 to 3 minutes. Puree in a blender or food processor. Blend in the butter, eggs, vanilla, and lemon rind until just combined. Transfer to a bowl.

Add the dry ingredients to the raisin mixture, mixing until well combined. Divide the dough into 7 equal portions, forming them into pancake shapes. Wrap separately and chill until firm enough to roll.

Preheat the oven to 400° F. Lightly grease 2 or 3 cookie sheets, rimless if possible.

On a lightly floured board or between sheets of waxed paper, roll out each portion of the flattened dough into a 9-inch circle. (Use a 9-inch cake pan as a guide.) With a wide spatula, lift the circles and place them on the prepared baking sheets. Bake for 10 minutes or until browned. Remove carefully with a spatula. Cool thoroughly on wire racks before assembling cake.

To make the prune filling, cook the prunes in the apple juice concentrate, adding water to barely cover. When they are tender, drain off the liquid and chop the prunes until minced. Add the lemon rind and nutmeg. Set aside.

APRICOT FILLING

4-1/2 cups dried apricots
1/2 cup frozen apple
  juice concentrate
Water

1/2 cup chopped walnuts

To make the apricot filling, cook the apricots in the apple juice concentrate, adding enough water to barely cover. When most of the liquid is absorbed, drain the fruit and chop until minced. Set aside.

To assemble, place 1 cookie round on a platter and spread with one-quarter of the apricot filling. Place a second round on top and spread with one-third of the prune filling. Repeat, alternating fillings, and top with the apricot filling. Sprinkle the chopped walnuts over the top.

Wrap the Celebration Cake securely with foil and age in the refrigerator for 6 to 7 days or in the freezer for 2 to 3 days. To serve, cut into 24 small wedges.

Yield: 24 servings

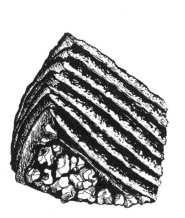 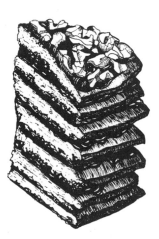

Seven-Layer Torte

Making this Seven-Layer Torte is a very entertaining ritual. Children enjoy putting one layer of goodies on top of another. During the holiday season we cut small squares of torte, place them in decorative paper casings and serve them as a confection-like version of fruitcake. Quite by accident, we discovered that Seven-Layer Torte is delicious if cut and served while it's still frozen.

1 cup rolled oats (noninstant)
1/4 cup melted butter or
  margarine
1 cup (8 ounces) chopped
  dates, well packed
1 cup chopped dried
  apricots
1-1/2 cups shredded wheat
  cereal or unsweetened
  flaked coconut
1 (8-ounce) can unsweetened
  crushed pineapple,
  well-drained
1 cup raisins
1-1/4 cups finely chopped
  nuts
2 eggs
2 tablespoons unbleached
  all-purpose flour
1/4 cup frozen apple
  juice concentrate, at
  room temperature
1-1/2 cups milk
1 teaspoon vanilla extract

Preheat the oven to 325° F. Lightly grease a 9-inch by 9-inch baking pan.

Layer 1. Combine the rolled oats and butter and spread over bottom of pan.

Layer 2. Sprinkle the dates over the rolled oats.

Layer 3. Sprinkle the apricots over the dates.

Layer 4. Sprinkle the shredded wheat or coconut over the apricots.

Layer 5. Sprinkle the crushed pineapple over the shredded wheat or coconut.

Layer 6. Sprinkle the raisins over the pineapple.

Layer 7. Sprinkle the chopped nuts over the raisins. Press all layers down gently.

In a bowl, beat the eggs lightly. Add the flour and beat well. Stir in the apple juice concentrate, milk, and vanilla. Pour the mixture evenly over torte. Bake for 30 to 35 minutes or until firm.

Cool the torte in its pan on a wire rack, then cut into squares.

Yield: 9 to 12 servings

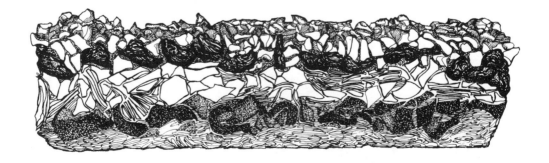

Swedish Apple Torte

Scandia, a fine restaurant in Los Angeles, inspired this torte. Serve it well-chilled with Light Milk Whip (page 210) and fresh berries when they are in season.

5 tablespoons butter or
  margarine
1 tablespoon frozen apple
  juice concentrate
3/4 cup finely ground dry
  bread crumbs
1/2 cup ground nuts
1/2 cup (4 ounces) ground
  dates, well packed
1-1/2 teaspoons cinnamon
1/2 teaspoon nutmeg
1/2 teaspoon allspice
3 cups (24-ounce jar)
  unsweetened chunky applesauce (or 1-1/2 recipes of
  Applesweet Applesauce,
  chunky style (page 187)
1 teaspoon cinnamon
1 teaspoon grated
  lemon rind

Preheat the oven to 325° F. Lightly grease a 1-quart baking dish or soufflé dish.

In a small saucepan, melt the butter with the apple juice concentrate.

In a bowl, combine the bread crumbs, nuts, dates, cinnamon, nutmeg, and allspice. Stir in the melted butter. Firmly press one-third of the crumbs in bottom of the baking dish. Combine the applesauce with the remaining 1 teaspoon cinnamon and lemon rind. Spread half the applesauce over the crumbs. Add another third of the crumbs and top with the remaining applesauce. Press on the remaining crumbs. Bake for 45 minutes.

Cool the torte in its pan on a wire rack, then refrigerate until thoroughly chilled. To serve, run a knife around edge of pan and invert the torte onto a serving platter.

Yield: 6 servings

Fig Torte

A trio of figs, almonds, and orange rind make this dessert a native Californian. The tiny fig seeds contribute a surprising amount of crunch. Try it with a glass of ice-cold milk.

3/4 cup ground almonds
1/2 cup finely ground dry
   bread crumbs
1 teaspoon cinnamon
1/2 teaspoon nutmeg
1/4 teaspoon cloves
1/4 teaspoon allspice
1/2 teaspoon baking powder
3/4 cup finely chopped
   dried figs (use scissors)
2 tablespoons finely grated
   orange rind
1/2 cup frozen apple juice
   concentrate, at room
   temperature
3/4 cup (6 ounces) chopped
   dates, well packed
5 egg yolks
1 teaspoon vanilla or
   brandy extract
5 egg whites, at room
   temperature
1/4 teaspoon cream
   of tartar
1/4 teaspoon salt

Preheat the oven to 325° F. Lightly grease and flour a 9-inch springform or pan with a removable bottom.

Combine the almonds, bread crumbs, cinnamon, nutmeg, cloves, allspice, and baking powder. Mix in the figs and orange rind.

In a blender or food processor, puree the apple juice concentrate and dates. Add the egg yolks and vanilla and continue to mix until well-blended. Transfer to a bowl and stir in the fig mixture.

Beat the egg whites until foamy. Add the cream of tartar and salt and continue to beat until stiff but not dry. Stir one-quarter of the egg whites into the batter, then gently fold in the rest. Immediately spoon into the prepared pan and bake for 45 to 60 minutes.

Cool the torte in its pan on a wire rack before releasing the sides.

Yield: 6 servings

Terra Bella Torte

An earthy raisin-filled torte that is flecked with bits of carrot and lemon peel.

1/2 cup (4 ounces) chopped dates, well packed

1 cup unsweetened apple butter (see page 202)

1 large whole lemon with peel, seeded and coarsely chopped

6 egg yolks, at room temperature

2/3 cup finely ground dry bread crumbs

2 cups finely ground almonds or filberts

1/2 teaspoon ground cloves

2-1/2 cups finely grated carrots, lightly packed

1 cup raisins, dark or golden

6 egg whites, at room temperature

1/4 teaspoon cream of tartar

1/4 teaspoon salt

Cream Cheese Topping (page 212) or Whipped Cheese Topping (page 211)

Preheat the oven to 375° F. Lightly grease a 9-inch springform or pan with a removable bottom.

In a blender or food processor, puree the dates with the apple butter and lemon. Blend in the egg yolks until just combined. Transfer to a large bowl.

Combine the bread crumbs with the ground nuts and cloves. Stir in the carrots and raisins. Add to the date mixture.

Beat the egg whites until foamy. Add the cream of tartar and salt and continue to beat until stiff but not dry. Stir one-quarter of the egg whites into the batter, then gently fold in the rest. Spoon the batter into the prepared pan. Bake for 55 to 60 minutes.

Cool the cake in its pan on a wire rack. Remove from pan when cool. Spread frosting over the top of the cake.

Yield: 10 to 12 servings

Walnut Torte

Walnut Torte is a moist, one-layer cake made without shortening and with ground nuts and crumbs instead of flour. It is adapted from a treasured recipe for Viennese nut torte. When nippy fall days arrive, we enjoy this dessert with a cup of Vienna roast coffee topped with a dollop of Light Milk Whip (page 210) and a dusting of cocoa.

2/3 cup (5 ounces) chopped dates, well packed
1/2 cup frozen apple juice concentrate, at room temperature
2 tablespoons frozen orange juice concentrate
2 tablespoons grated orange rind
3 egg yolks
1 teaspoon vanilla extract
1-1/2 cups toasted and finely ground walnuts
1/2 cup finely ground dry bread crumbs
3 egg whites, at room temperature
1/4 teaspoon cream of tartar
1/4 teaspoon salt

Preheat the oven to 350° F. Lightly grease and flour an 8-inch springform or pan with a removable bottom.

In a blender or food processor, puree the dates, apple juice concentrate, and orange juice concentrate. Add the orange rind, egg yolks, and vanilla, mixing until well-blended. Transfer to a bowl. Stir in the walnuts and bread crumbs.

Beat the egg whites until foamy. Add the cream of tartar and salt and continue to beat until stiff but not dry. Stir one-quarter of the egg whites into the date-nut mixture, then gently fold in the rest. Spoon into the prepared pan. Bake for 30 minutes.

Cool the torte in its pan on a wire rack. Remove from the pan when cool.

Yield: 6 servings

Four Seasons Torte

A spectacular torte that makes use of fruit from any of the four seasons. It makes a marvelous addition to a dessert buffet. Or cut it into wedges and serve it as a cookie. The base is a flavorful almond crust mildly sweetened with dates. An assortment of fresh fruit decorates the top of the cake in whatever combination pleases you. In spring, we suggest using fruits such as strawberries, melons, kiwi, or papaya; in summer, try peaches, nectarines, apricots, mangoes, grapes, cherries, or berries. In fall and winter, our favorites are pears, pineapple, or oranges. (Allow 1 to 2 hours for the fruits to steep in the apple juice.)

TOPPING

1 cup unsweetened fruit
  (fresh, frozen and defrosted,
  or canned), peeled, pitted,
  and sliced as desired
1 teaspoon lemon juice
1/3 cup frozen apple juice
  concentrate, at room
  temperature

CAKE

1 cup whole almonds
1/2 cup (4 ounces) chopped
  dates, well packed
1/4 cup butter or margarine,
  at room temperature
2 eggs
1/2 teaspoon almond extract
2 tablespoons unbleached
  all-purpose flour
Toasted sliced almonds

To make the topping, drain any excess juice from the fruits and combine the fruits in a bowl. Toss with the lemon juice and apple juice concentrate. Cover and refrigerate.

Preheat the oven to 325° F. Lightly grease and flour a 9-inch springform or pan with a removable bottom.

In a food processor or food chopper, grind the whole almonds and dates. Place in a bowl and mix in the butter. Beat in the eggs, one at a time, beating well after each addition. Stir in the almond extract and the flour. Spread the mixture into the prepared pan. Bake for 20 to 25 minutes, or until golden.

Cool the torte in its pan on a wire rack. Remove from the pan when cool and place on a serving plate. About an hour before serving, remove the fruit from the juice with a slotted spoon. Arrange it in concentric circles on top of the torte. Place the juice in a small saucepan and bring to a boil. Stir the boiling mixture until it is slightly thickened, 2 to 3 minutes. Spoon the juice over the fruit. Sprinkle the toasted almonds over the top of the torte and serve.

Store leftover torte in the refrigerator. Only the cake layer should be frozen.

Yield: 6 servings

Black and White Cheesecake

Cheesecake buffs are known to have very particular preferences. We believe this recipe with its creamy white filling and shiny black poppy seed topping will satisfy the purists as well as the innovators. The first slice reveals a dramatic contrast of texture and color.

CRUMB CRUST

1 cup finely ground dry
  bread crumbs
1/4 teaspoon nutmeg
1/4 cup chopped nuts
3 tablespoons butter or
  margarine, melted

POPPY SEED LAYER

1 cup (5 ounces) poppy seeds
3/4 cup very finely
  chopped raisins
1/2 cup frozen apple
  juice concentrate
1 cup low-fat milk
1 tablespoon grated
  lemon rind
2 teaspoons cornstarch
1/4 cup orange juice
1/2 teaspoon vanilla extract

CHEESE FILLING

12 ounces low-fat cream
  cheese, at room
  temperature
1/3 cup frozen apple juice
  concentrate, at room
  temperature
1-1/2 teaspoons vanilla
  extract
2 eggs, lightly beaten
1/2 cup finely chopped nuts

To make the crumb crust, measure the crumbs, nutmeg, and nuts into a blender or food processor and whirl them together until the nuts are ground. Remove the mixture to a bowl and stir in the melted butter. Press into the bottom and slightly up the sides of an 8-inch springform or pan with a removable bottom.

To make the poppy seed layer, combine the poppy seeds, raisins, apple juice concentrate, milk, and lemon rind in a small saucepan. Simmer for 10 minutes. Dissolve the cornstarch in the orange juice and add to the poppy seed mixture along with the vanilla and bring to a boil, stirring constantly until slightly thickened.

Drop spoonfuls of the poppy seed mixture carefully over crust, smoothing it with the back of the spoon.

Preheat the oven to 325° F.

To prepare the cheese filling, blend the cream cheese, frozen apple juice concentrate, and vanilla together. Stir in the beaten eggs, beating until smooth. Spread the mixture over the poppy seed layer. Sprinkle with the chopped nuts. Bake for 40 minutes or until firm.

Cool the cheesecake in its pan on a wire rack. Remove from pan when cool and chill until served.

Yield: 8 servings

Tofu-Banana-Pineapple Cheesecake

Tofu stands in for the usual cream cheese in this recipe. The flavor is fruity, with crushed pineapple adding a subtle chewiness to the otherwise silken texture. Cheesecake purists will enjoy this while grumbling that cheesecake without cheese could never be worthy of the name.

CRUMB CRUST

1-1/4 cups finely ground dry bread crumbs
1 teaspoon cinnamon
1/4 cup chopped nuts
3 tablespoons butter or margarine, melted
2 teaspoons frozen apple juice concentrate at room temperature

FILLING

1/2 cup (4 ounces) chopped dates, well packed
1/3 cup frozen apple juice concentrate, at room temperature
2 eggs
1 pound tofu, drained and cubed
2 very ripe bananas, cut into chunks
1 tablespoon grated lemon rind
1 tablespoon lemon juice
2 teaspoons vanilla extract
1 (20-ounce) can unsweetened crushed pineapple, with juice pressed out

Preheat the oven to 325° F.

To make the crust, combine the crumbs, cinnamon, and nuts in a blender or food processor and whirl them together until the nuts are ground. Remove the mixture to a bowl and stir in the melted butter and apple juice concentrate. Press into the bottom and slightly up the sides of a 9-inch springform or pan with a removable bottom.

To make the filling, puree the dates, apple juice concentrate, and eggs in a blender or food processor. Add all the remaining ingredients, except the pineapple, and continue to blend, in batches if necessary, until smooth. Pour the mixture into a bowl and stir in the crushed pineapple. Pour into the crust and bake for 1 hour.

Cool the cheesecake in its pan on a wire rack. Remove from the pan when cool and chill until served. Store leftover cheesecake in the refrigerator.

Yield: 8 servings

Currant Cheesecake with Yogurt Topping

Try serving serve this currant-studded cheesecake with wild blackberry tea. As a shortcut, substitute 1/4 cup nonsweetened commercial fruit yogurt mixed with 2 ounces of cream cheese for the topping recipe below.

CRUMB CRUST

1 cup finely ground dry
  bread crumbs
1/4 teaspoon nutmeg
1/4 cup chopped nuts
3 tablespoons butter or
  margarine, melted

FILLING

6 ounces low-fat cream
  cheese, at room
  temperature
1/2 cup low-fat sour cream
2 egg yolks
1/4 cup frozen apple juice
  concentrate, at room
  temperature
1 teaspoon grated
  lemon rind
1 teaspoon lemon juice
1 teaspoon vanilla extract
3 tablespoons dried
  currants tossed with
  1 teaspoon flour
2 egg whites, at room
  temperature
1/8 teaspoon cream
  of tartar
1/8 teaspoon salt

To make the crust, combine the crumbs, nutmeg, and nuts in a blender or food processor and whirl them together until the nuts are ground. Remove the mixture to a bowl and stir in the the melted butter. Press into the bottom and slightly up the sides of an 8-inch springform or pan with a removable bottom.

Preheat the oven to 325° F.

To make the filling, blend the 6 ounces of the cream cheese, sour cream, and egg yolks in a blender or food processor. Add the apple juice concentrate, lemon rind, lemon juice, and vanilla and continue to blend until well-combined. Transfer to a bowl and stir in the currants.

Beat the egg whites until foamy. Add the cream of tartar and salt and continue to beat until stiff but not dry. Stir one-quarter of the egg whites into the cheese mixture, then gently fold in the rest. Spoon into the crust and bake for 45 minutes. Turn off the heat and allow the cheesecake to remain in the oven for 40 minutes before opening the door.

Cool the cheesecake in its pan on a wire rack. Remove from the pan when cool and chill until served.

TOPPING

2 tablespoons (1 ounce) chopped dates, well packed
1 tablespoon chopped nuts
1/4 cup plain nonfat yogurt
2 ounces low-fat cream cheese
1 teaspoon frozen apple juice concentrate
1/4 teaspoon lemon or vanilla extract
2 to 3 tablespoons dried currants

To make the topping, puree the dates, nuts, yogurt, cream cheese, frozen apple juice concentrate, and lemon extract in a blender or food processor. Spread over the top of chilled cheesecake. Sprinkle the remaining 2 to 3 tablespoons currants over the top of the cheesecake.

Yield: 6 servings

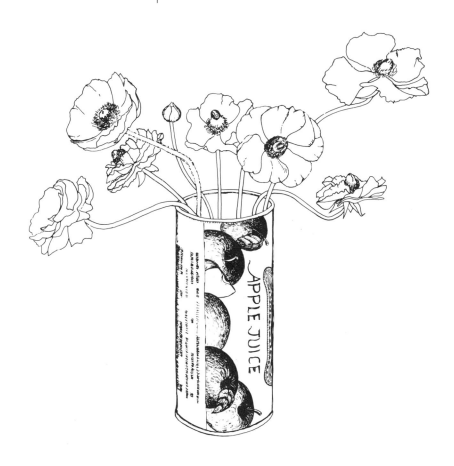

Fruit-Topped Cottage Cheesecake

For devotees of less-rich desserts, we are delighted to offer a luxurious cheesecake made with cottage cheese. Artfully arrange fresh fruit on top and you will have an elegant offering for any special occasion.

CRUMB CRUST

1-1/4 cups finely ground dry
  bread crumbs
1/4 teaspoon nutmeg
1/4 cup chopped nuts
3 tablespoons butter or
  margarine, melted
2 teaspoons frozen apple
  juice concentrate, at room
  temperature

FILLING

1/2 cup coarsely chopped
  golden raisins
1/2 cup frozen apple juice
  concentrate
1/4 cup water
4 cups low-fat cottage cheese
4 eggs
1/4 cup unbleached all-
  purpose flour
1/4 cup nonfat yogurt or
  low-fat sour cream
2 teaspoons grated
  lemon rind
1 tablespoon lemon juice
1 teaspoon vanilla extract

TOPPING

1 cup unsweetened sliced
  fruit, such as nectarines,
  peaches, pears, or whole
  blueberries, blackberries,
  raspberries
Melba Sauce (page 205)
  (optional)

Preheat the oven to 275° F.

To make the crust, measure the crumbs, nutmeg, and nuts into a blender or food processor and whirl them together until the nuts are ground. Remove the mixture to a bowl and stir in the melted butter. Press into the bottom and slightly up the sides of a 9-inch springform or pan with a removable bottom.

To make the filling, combine the raisins with the apple juice concentrate and water in a small saucepan. Simmer until the raisins are slightly softened, 2 to 3 minutes. Puree in a blender or food processor. Cool slightly before adding the cottage cheese. Blend until smooth. Continue to blend, in batches if necessary, adding the eggs, flour, yogurt, lemon rind, lemon juice, and vanilla. Pour the mixture into the crust and bake for 1-1/2 to 1-3/4 hours, or until firm.

Cool the cheesecake in its pan on a wire rack. Remove from pan when cool and chill. Just before serving, arrange the fruit on top of the cheesecake. Glaze with the Melba Sauce, if desired. Store leftover cheesecake in the refrigerator.

Yield: 8 servings

Crisps, Cobblers, Pies, & Tarts

M any of the recipes in this chapter are designed to take advantage of the changing seasons. When fresh fruit is at its peak, there is always peach, berry, and even cantaloupe pie. As harvest season arrives, there are the Thanksgiving favorites: apple, pumpkin, and mince pie. Harvest Fruit Crisp and Crumble-Topped Pear Crisp are simple creations that feature the fruits most abundant in fall and early winter: apples and pears. When Jack Frost taps at the windowpane, chase away the chill with a bubbling hot Cranberry, Apple, 'n' Raisin Cobbler. Each serving fills the dish with cranberry-stained, rosy red fruit.

The fruit you choose for these pies and desserts should be of high quality and perfectly ripe. The taste and aroma of your fruit will be reflected back to you in your first bite. If you can't find good quality fruit, choose a recipe that doesn't require fresh fruit, such as a Glazed Cream Cheese Pie or a Prune Tart.

Here are some tips for successful pie baking and crust making. One guideline always bears repeating: Preheat your oven and be certain it is at the correct temperature before putting in anything to bake.

Flour, shortening, and liquid are the ingredients basic to pastry making. Start with cold ingredients, work quickly, and avoid adding warmth to the dough by handling it as little as possible. You can tell when dough is at its optimum working temperature by its plasticity.

For pastry making, you will want to use unbleached all-purpose flour or whole wheat pastry flour. These are soft wheat flours that make a tender crust.

While the nutty flavor of whole wheat complements many fillings, whole wheat increases the heaviness of the crust. You may have to experiment until you find the proportion of white to whole wheat flour you prefer. Whole wheat pastry flour is available at food coops and natural foods stores.

The shortening you choose also determines the texture, taste, and handling quality of your pastry. Solid fats, such as butter, margarine, and cream cheese, make a pastry either tender or flaky, depending on your mixing technique. For a tender crust, use a pastry blender or 2 knives to cut in the shortening until the mixture resembles cornmeal. If you leave pea-size bits of shortening in the pastry, the pastry will be flaky. Crusts made with vegetable oil are distinctively crisp rather than tender or flaky, and dough made with oil is not as pliable as dough made with solid shortening. There are recipes for both oil and solid shortening crusts at the end of this chapter, as well as pastry doughs made with yogurt, cottage cheese, almonds, and crumbs.

A pastry recipe can only approximate the amount of liquid required because the moisture content of the flour varies with the temperature and humidity. Don't be surprised if you have to depart from a recipe to get the proper working consistency. What you are looking for is a mixture that looks like coarse meal. Add water or liquid at the beginning of the mixing process, using the smaller amount called for in the recipe (except for oil doughs, where the liquid goes in all at once). Consider if you can gather the dough into a smooth ball. If you doubt it, add more liquid, a teaspoon at a time, until you can form the dough into a smooth ball that isn't sticky. Don't manipulate the dough more than necessary.

Once you have gathered the dough into a ball, shape it into a disk or pancake. If time permits, wrap and refrigerate it briefly (particularly if the kitchen is warm); if you can chill it for several hours or overnight that is even better. Chilling allows the flour to absorb moisture and expand, making it easier to handle, less apt to shrink in the pie pan, and more tender. Well-chilled dough is stiff and may need to soften slightly at room temperature for a few minutes before you roll it.

To help prevent a soggy bottom crust, you may want to brush the unbaked pie shell with egg white and sprinkle with a little of the spice used in the filling. Once baking is completed, remove the pies, tarts, cobblers, and crisps to wire racks to allow air to circulate evenly around them.

Unless you serve these desserts within a few hours of baking, cool the dessert, then wrap and refrigerate or freeze it.

Unbaked pie dough freezes well. Shape it into a thick pancake, wrap, and freeze it. Thaw it still wrapped, at room temperature, until it is soft enough to handle. You can also freeze already formed pie shells. Bake frozen pie shells without thawing.

To freeze baked pie shells, wrap well. Handle carefully because the pie shells are fragile. Once frozen, the pie shells are strong enough to be removed from the pans and wrapped in stacks. If tightly sealed, pastry can be frozen for at least 3 months. Once they have thawed, refresh baked pie shells in a 300° F. oven for 5 minutes.

Crumb crusts also freeze very well.

Harvest Fruit Crisp

Choose fruit that is sweet and flavorful as there is no additional sweetener in this dessert.

TOPPING

1/2 cup finely chopped raisins
1/2 cup chopped walnuts
1 cup rolled oats (noninstant)
1/4 cup unbleached all-
   purpose or whole wheat
   pastry flour
1/4 teaspoon nutmeg
1/4 cup butter or margarine,
   at room temperature

FILLING

3 large apples, cored and
   sliced into eighths
2 large pears, peeled
   (optional) and sliced
1-1/2 cups sweet seedless
   grapes
2 teaspoons grated
   lemon rind
2 tablespoons lemon juice
1/2 teaspoon cardamom or
   allspice

To make the topping, blend all the ingredients with a fork or your fingers until combined. Set aside.

Preheat the oven to 350° F. Lightly grease a 9-inch pie plate.

To make the filling, toss the apples, pears, and grapes with the lemon rind, lemon juice, and cardamom. Arrange in the prepared pie plate and cover with the topping. Bake for 50 minutes.

Cool the crisp slightly on a wire rack. Serve while still warm.

Yield: 6 servings

Crumble-Topped Pear Crisp

This dessert is well suited for a potluck. It travels well and is so easy to make. As a bonus, the perfume of pears and nutmeg lingers throughout the house long after the baking is done.

Fruit crisps can be prepared and refrigerated for up to 24 hours before baking. Bake during dinner and serve hot and steaming from the oven.

TOPPING

1/4 cup finely ground dry bread crumbs

1/4 cup chopped walnuts

1/4 cup (2 ounces) chopped dates, well packed

3 tablespoons unsweetened shredded coconut

2 tablespoons unbleached all-purpose flour

2 tablespoons butter, melted

1 teaspoon cinnamon

1/2 teaspoon nutmeg

1 tablespoon frozen apple juice concentrate, at room temperature

FILLING

4 to 6 ripe pears, peeled (optional) and sliced

2 tablespoons frozen apple juice concentrate, at room temperature

2 tablespoons flour

1 tablespoon grated lemon rind

1 teaspoon nutmeg

1/2 cup low-fat sour cream (optional)

To make the topping, blend all the ingredients with a fork or fingers until combined. Set aside.

Preheat the oven to 350° F. Lightly grease a 9-inch pie plate.

To make the filling, toss the pears with the apple juice concentrate. Stir in the flour, lemon rind, nutmeg, and sour cream, if used. Arrange the fruit in the prepared pie plate and cover with the topping. Bake for 45 minutes.

Cool on a wire rack. Serve warm or at room temperature.

Yield: 6 servings

Cranberry, Apple, and Raisin Cobbler

Once the holiday season is past, raw cranberries disappear from the supermarket. It's a good idea to freeze a few packages to insure that you can make a bubbly hot cobbler any time of the year. This recipe is also delicious when made with fresh or frozen unsweetened blueberries. The filling can be prepared 1 day ahead.

FILLING

2 cups fresh cranberries
2/3 cup raisins
2/3 cup frozen apple juice
  concentrate
4 apples, peeled (optional)
  and coarsely chopped
  (about 4 cups)

COBBLER TOPPING

1-1/4 cups unbleached
  all-purpose flour (or
  use half whole wheat
  pastry flour)
1-1/2 teaspoons baking
  powder
1/4 teaspoon salt
1/2 teaspoon cinnamon
3 ounces low-fat cream
  cheese
2 tablespoons butter or
  margarine
1 egg, slightly beaten
3 tablespoons milk
1/4 cup frozen apple
  juice concentrate, at
  room temperature
1 teaspoon butter or
  margarine, melted

Lightly grease a 10-inch pie plate or 1-1/2-quart casserole.

To make the filling, combine the cranberries, raisins, and apple juice concentrate in a saucepan. Bring to a boil, then simmer until the cranberries burst. Remove to a bowl and add the chopped apples. Spoon the mixture into the prepared pie plate. Bring to room temperature if made ahead and refrigerated.

Preheat the oven to 450° F.

To make the topping, sift together the flour, baking powder, salt, and cinnamon. Add the cream cheese and butter, cutting them in with a pastry blender or two knives until the mixture resembles coarse cornmeal. Combine the egg, milk, and apple juice concentrate. Stir into the flour mixture. If the dough is too sticky, add more flour. Stir for about 20 seconds. Spoon the dough over the top of the fruit mixture. Brush the top with melted butter. Bake for 20 minutes.

Cool slightly on a wire rack. Serve while still warm.

Yield: 6 servings

Cranberry Surprise

This cousin to the dessert omelet is wonderful served as breakfast or brunch fare. An omelet-like batter is poured under and over the fruit. After it's baked, plump crimson portions of the cranberries pop out of the golden crust. This recipe can also be made using 1 cup pitted black cherries.

1 cup cranberries

2 tablespoons frozen apple juice concentrate

1-1/2 teaspoons grated orange rind

1/4 cup (2 ounces) chopped dates, well packed

1/2 cup low-fat milk

1/2 cup frozen apple juice concentrate, at room temperature

4 eggs

1/2 teaspoon vanilla extract

1/8 teaspoon salt

Preheat the oven to 400° F. Lightly grease a 10-inch pie plate.

Toss the cranberries with the 2 tablespoons apple juice concentrate and orange rind. Set aside.

In a blender or food processor, puree the dates with the milk and the remaining 1/2 cup apple juice concentrate. Add the eggs, vanilla, and salt, blending until just combined. Pour 1 cup of the batter into the prepared pie plate. Bake for 4 minutes. Remove from the oven and spoon the cranberry mixture evenly over the surface. Pour the remaining batter over. Bake for 20 to 25 minutes. Serve warm.

Yield: 6 servings

Berry Shortcake

Shortcake is the classic way to celebrate summer's berry season and, if there are berries in the freezer, it's possible to make an out-of-season shortcake surprise.

BERRY FILLING

4 cups unsweetened frozen
  berries
1/3 cup frozen apple juice
  concentrate, at room
  temperature
1/2 cup chopped dried
  apples

SHORTCAKE

2 cups unbleached all-
  purpose or whole wheat
  pastry flour
1 tablespoon baking powder
1/4 teaspoon salt
3 ounces low-fat cream
  cheese
2 tablespoons butter or
  margarine
1 egg, slightly beaten
1/4 cup low-fat milk
1/4 cup frozen apple juice
  concentrate, at room
  temperature
2 teaspoons butter or
  margarine, melted
Light Milk Whip (page 210)
Grated nutmeg

To make the filling, heat the berries with the apple juice concentrate and apples in a small saucepan. Bring to a boil, reduce the heat, and simmer, uncovered, until the fruits are softened. The filling can prepared ahead and refrigerated. Reheat before serving.

Preheat the oven to 450° F. Lightly grease a cookie sheet.

To make the shortcake, sift together the flour, baking powder, and salt. Cut in the cream cheese and butter with a pastry blender or 2 knives until the mixture resembles coarse cornmeal. Combine the egg, milk, and apple juice concentrate. Gradually stir into the flour mixture. Knead the dough for about 20 seconds. Divide into 4 equal parts, patting each into a 5-inch pancake. Place on the greased baking sheet, brushing the tops with the melted butter. Bake for 20 minutes or until golden.

Prepare the Light Milk Whip while the shortcakes are baking.

Just before serving, split the hot shortcakes in half. Spoon the warm berry mixture over the bottom half of each shortcake. Cover the berries with a spoonful of the Light Milk Whip. Gently press on the top short-cake layer. Spoon over the remaining berries and another spoonful of topping. Sprinkle lightly with nutmeg. Serve immediately.

Yield: 4 servings

Fresh Strawberry Pie Glacé

This pie glistens like a precious ruby in a crisp, cookie-like almond pastry. If you feel like adding a garnish, try a dusting of finely chopped pistachio nuts. They add an unexpected color accent.

ALMOND PIE SHELL

1/4 cup butter or margarine, at room temperature
2 tablespoons frozen apple juice concentrate, at room temperature
1/4 cup finely ground almonds
1/2 teaspoon almond extract
1 teaspoon grated lemon rind
1 egg white
1 cup unbleached all-purpose flour (or use half whole wheat pastry flour)

FILLING

5 cups fresh strawberries, washed, hulled, and drained
1/2 cup frozen apple juice concentrate
1/4 cup water
1-1/2 tablespoons cornstarch
2 tablespoons water
1 teaspoon finely chopped unsalted pistachio nuts (optional)

To prepare the pie shell, lightly grease a 9-inch pie plate.

With an electric mixer, cream together the butter, apple juice concentrate, almonds, almond extract, and lemon rind. Add the egg white and beat at high speed until combined. Add the flour gradually, beating until smooth. Press into the pie plate with the back of a spoon, covering the bottom and sides. Chill in the refrigerator for 15 minutes.

Preheat the oven to 325° F. Bake for 15 minutes, or until golden brown. Set aside to cool.

To prepare the filling, crush 1 cup of the softest strawberries. Place in a small saucepan with the apple juice concentrate and 1/4 cup water. Bring to a boil, reduce the heat, and simmer for 5 minutes. Strain to collect the liquid, reserving the pulp for another use.

Return the strained juices to the saucepan and bring to a boil. Dissolve the cornstarch in the remaining 2 tablespoons water. Stir into the saucepan and boil for 1 minute, stirring constantly until the mixture is thickened and clear. Remove from the heat.

Fill the cooled pie shell with the remaining 4 cups whole strawberries. Spoon the thickened berry glaze over the fruit. Sprinkle with the nuts. Chill and serve cold.

Yield: 6 servings

Fresh Peach Pie with Melba Glaze

Bright yellow peaches peeking through a shiny dark glaze. This pie is gorgeous!

9-inch pie shell, baked
  (pages 72 and 74)
6 cups peeled, sliced, yellow
  freestone peaches
1 tablespoon lemon juice
2 cups pitted black cherries
  or raspberries (fresh or
  unsweetened canned or
  frozen and defrosted)
1/4 cup frozen apple juice
  concentrate
1/4 cup orange juice
1/4 teaspoon cinnamon
1 tablespoon cornstarch
2 tablespoons orange juice
1 teaspoon brandy extract
  (optional)

Prepare the pie shell and set aside to cool.

In a bowl, toss the peaches with the lemon juice. Set aside.

In a small saucepan, combine the cherries with the apple juice concentrate and orange juice. Bring to a boil, reduce the heat, and simmer for 5 minutes until the fruit is very soft. Puree in a blender or food processor. Strain and discard any pulp. Return the strained juices to the saucepan and bring to a boil. Dissolve the cornstarch in the 2 tablespoons orange juice. Add to the cherry mixture, stirring constantly until the glaze is thickened. Remove from the heat and stir in the brandy extract if used. Allow to cool slightly.

Drain the peaches and arrange them in the pie shell. Spoon the glaze over the fruit. Chill until served.

Yield: 6 servings

Cantaloupe Pie

When you are in the mood for something refreshing and light, make Cantaloupe Pie. Any melon in season will do, the riper the better. Instead of almond, other extracts such as rum or brandy are also good. You will need to steep the fruit in juice for an hour before putting the pie together. This intensifies the melon's highly perfumed flavor.

9-inch pie shell, baked
  (pages 72 and 74)
1 1/2 cups diced cantaloupe
1-1/2 tablespoons lemon juice
1/2 cup frozen apple juice
  concentrate
1 tablespoon frozen orange
  juice concentrate
3 tablespoons cornstarch
Pinch salt
1/4 teaspoon almond extract
Mint leaves

Prepare the pie shell and set aside to cool.

Combine the cantaloupe, lemon juice, apple juice concentrate, and orange juice concentrate. Let stand for 1 hour to allow the fruit to steep in the juices.

Drain the fruit and measure the juice. Add enough water to make 1-1/2 cups. Make a paste with the cornstarch and a few tablespoons of the juice. Mix until smooth, then stir in the remaining juice. In a small saucepan, slowly bring the mixture to a boil; boil for 1 minute, stirring constantly until thickened. Remove from the heat and stir in the salt and almond extract. Fold in the well-drained fruit. Cool slightly. Spoon into the pie shell and chill. Just before serving, decorate with the mint leaves.

Yield: 6 servings

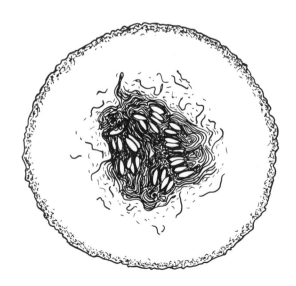

Lemon Loop Pie

With its garnish of curled and twisted lemon peel, this pie makes a big hit when presented at the table. There's a tart, clean edge to the flavor which complements any menu. Lemon Loop Pie can be prepared up to 1 day ahead or served without a crust as Lemon Loop Pudding. To serve as a pie, you will need a 10-inch pie plate. To serve crustless as a pudding, use 8 small dessert dishes.

CRUMB CRUST

1-1/2 cups finely ground dry
  bread crumbs
1/2 teaspoon cinnamon
1 teaspoon grated lemon rind
1/4 cup chopped nuts
3 tablespoons butter or
  margarine, melted
2 teaspoons frozen apple
  juice concentrate, at room
  temperature

FILLING

2 envelopes unflavored
  gelatin
1/2 cup lemon juice
3/4 cup frozen apple juice
  concentrate
2 egg whites
2 tablespoons grated
  lemon rind
8 ounces low-fat cream
  cheese, cut into cubes
3/4 cup low-fat milk
3/4 cup cracked ice
2 to 3 lemons

Preheat the oven to 350° F.

To prepare the crust, combine the crumbs, cinnamon, lemon rind, and nuts in a blender or food processor and whirl them together until the nuts are ground. Remove the mixture to a bowl and stir in the melted butter and apple juice concentrate. Press into the bottom and up the sides of a 10-inch pie plate. Chill until needed.

To make the filling, sprinkle the gelatin over the lemon juice in a blender or food processor and let stand for 3 minutes. Heat the apple juice concentrate until it comes to a boil. Add to the softened gelatin and blend until the gelatin is dissolved. Blend in the egg whites and lemon rind. Continue blending as you add the cream cheese and milk. Finally, add the cracked ice and blend until it dissolves. Let the mixture stand for a few minutes, then pour into the crumb crust or 8 dessert dishes. Chill until firm, about 2 hours.

To garnish, make lemon loops with a sharp paring knife or a citrus stripper. To use a knife, make crosswise cuts into the peel, 1/8 inch apart, around the middle of several lemons. Slash through the cuts at one point and cut the strips of peel away from the pulp. To use a citrus stripper, carve around each lemon making a continuous strip of peel. Once you have the strips, cut them into 4-inch lengths and tie them loosely into loops. Decorate the pie with 8 lemon loops, 1 for each serving.

Yield: 6 servings

Blueberry Pie

This pie may bring back childhood memories of blueberry picking — tin pails brim full — and at the end of the day, freshly made pies with thick whipped cream from grandmother's kitchen. Our version uses uncooked berries for a very fresh berry flavor.

9-inch pie shell, baked
  (pages 72 and 74)
4 cups blueberries (fresh or
  unsweetened frozen and
  defrosted)
1/4 cup frozen apple juice
  concentrate
1/4 cup water
1 teaspoon grated lemon rind
1 teaspoon lemon juice
1/2 teaspoon cinnamon
1-1/2 tablespoons cornstarch
1/4 cup unsweetened apple
  or grape juice

Prepare the pie shell and set aside to cool.

Drain the blueberries thoroughly. Spread 2 cups of the berries on a towel to dry while preparing the glaze.

In a saucepan, combine the remaining 2 cups blueberries with apple juice concentrate, water, lemon rind, lemon juice, and cinnamon. Bring to a boil. Dissolve the cornstarch in the apple juice. Add to the saucepan and boil for 1 minute, stirring gently until thickened.

Place the uncooked berries in the pie shell. Spoon the thickened berry glaze over the fruit. Chill until served.

Yield: 6 servings

Coconut-Crusted Banana Cream Pie

This tropical pie is perfect for a summer barbecue or alfresco supper.

COCONUT CRUST

- 3 tablespoons butter or margarine
- 2 tablespoons frozen apple juice concentrate
- 2 cups unsweetened shredded coconut

To make the crust, lightly grease a 9-inch pie plate. In a small skillet, melt the butter with the apple juice concentrate. Stir in coconut and sauté over low heat, stirring until the coconut is golden brown and the liquid is absorbed. With a spoon, press the mixture on the bottom and up the sides of the pie plate. Chill while preparing the filling.

FILLING

2 cups low-fat milk
3 tablespoons cornstarch
2 teaspoons unbleached all-
   purpose flour
1/8 teaspoon salt
1/3 cup frozen apple juice
   concentrate, at room
   temperature
3 egg yolks
2 teaspoons grated
   orange rind
2 teaspoons vanilla extract
3 ripe bananas

In a heavy-bottomed saucepan, heat the milk just until warmed. Mix the cornstarch, flour, and salt in a bowl. Add the milk slowly to the cornstarch mixture, stirring until smooth. Return the mixture to the saucepan and bring to a boil. Boil for 1 minute, stirring constantly until thickened. Remove from the heat. Stir in the apple juice concentrate.

With a fork, lightly beat the egg yolks. Stir 3 table-spoons of the milk mixture into the egg yolks, then gradually stir the yolks into the remaining hot milk in the saucepan. Cook over low heat, stirring constantly until thickened, about 2 minutes. Remove from the heat and stir in the orange rind and vanilla. Transfer to a bowl. Cover the surface of the pudding with plastic wrap to prevent a skin from forming and cool to room temperature.

Slice 2-1/2 bananas, reserving the remaining half of the third banana for the garnish. Arrange some of the slices on bottom of crust. Cover with half of cooled pudding mixture. Layer the remaining banana slices and top with the rest of pudding. Chill for at least 2 hours. Just before serving, slice the remaining banana half over the top.

Yield: 6 servings

Pumpkin Cloud Pie

This is pumpkin pie with wings. The filling can be served in a pie shell, in individual tarts, or as a pudding in custard cups.

10-inch pie shell, baked
  (pages 72 and 74) or
  baked tartlet shells
  (pages 73 and 75)
1 envelope unflavored
  gelatin
1/4 cup frozen apple juice
  concentrate, at room
  temperature
3 egg yolks, lightly beaten
1-1/2 cups canned or
  cooked and strained
  pumpkin
1/2 cup low-fat evaporated
  milk
3/4 cup frozen apple juice
  concentrate, at room
  temperature
1/4 teaspoon salt
1-1/2 teaspoons cinnamon
1 teaspoon ginger
1/2 teaspoon nutmeg
3 egg whites, at room
  temperature
1/4 teaspoon cream
  of tartar
1/8 teaspoon salt
2 tablespoons frozen apple
  juice concentrate, at room
  temperature
1 teaspoon rum extract

Prepare the pie shell or tartlet shells and set aside.

Sprinkle the gelatin over the 1/4 cup apple juice concentrate and set aside.

Stir together the egg yolks, pumpkin, milk, 3/4 cup apple juice concentrate, salt, and spices in the top of a double boiler or heavy saucepan. Cook until thickened, 5 to 7 minutes, stirring frequently. Stir in the softened gelatin until completely dissolved and set aside to cool.

Beat the egg whites until foamy. Add the cream of tartar and salt. Continue beating until stiff but not dry. Beat in the remaining 2 tablespoons apple juice concentrate and rum extract. Stir one-quarter of the beaten whites into the pumpkin mixture, then gently fold in the rest. Spoon into the baked pie shell, tartlet shells, or 6 custard cups. Serve when thoroughly chilled.

Yield: 6 servings

Pumpkin Pie

You might want to substitute cooked fresh pumpkin for the canned, or you can use the sweet orange flesh of a winter squash, such as butternut or hubbard. You will need to press the cooked flesh through a food mill or ricer to remove the stringy fibers. If you don't want to make a pie crust, serve the filling in dessert dishes as a pudding.

9-inch pie shell, with a high fluted edge (pages 72 and 74), unbaked
1/2 cup (4 ounces) coarsely chopped dates, well packed
6 tablespoons frozen apple juice concentrate, at room temperature
1-1/2 tablespoons grated orange rind
2 eggs
1-1/2 cups canned pumpkin
3/4 cup low-fat evaporated milk
1 teaspoon vanilla extract
1-1/2 teaspoons cinnamon
1/2 teaspoon ginger
1/8 teaspoon cloves
1/4 teaspoon salt
1 cup toasted pecan halves

Preheat the oven to 350° F. Prepare the pie shell and refrigerate.

In a blender or food processor, puree the dates, apple juice concentrate, and orange rind. Add the eggs and blend until just combined.

Combine the pumpkin with the evaporated milk, vanilla, spices, and salt. Add the date and apple juice mixture and stir until smooth. Pour into the pie shell. Bake for 1 to 1-1/4 hours, or until firm.

Cool the pie on a wire rack. Just before serving, garnish with toasted pecans arranged in concentric circles on top of the pie. Serve warm or chilled.

Yield: 6 servings

Golden Delicious Apple Pie

Golden delicious apples are our first choice for this fragrant pie, but other kinds of apple can be used.

PIE

Pastry for 1 double-crusted
  9-inch or 10-inch pie
  (pages 72 and 74), chilled
8 golden delicious apples,
  peeled (optional) and sliced
1 tablespoon frozen apple
  juice concentrate
1 tablespoon unbleached
  all-purpose flour
1/2 to 1 teaspoon cinnamon
1/4 teaspoon nutmeg
1/4 teaspoon cloves
1 tablespoon grated
  lemon rind
2 tablespoons butter or
  margarine, diced

GLAZE

1 egg yolk
1 teaspoon frozen apple
  juice concentrate, at room
  temperature

Roll out the large half of the chilled dough and line a 9-inch pie plate, leaving a 1-inch overhang. Refrigerate while you prepare the filling.

Toss the apples with the apple juice concentrate. Stir in the flour, spices, and lemon rind. Set aside.

Preheat the oven to 425° F.

Arrange the apples in the lined pie pan and dot with the diced butter. Roll out the remaining dough into a 10-inch round and place over the filling. Fold the edge of the top crust under the edge of the bottom crust. Press together to seal. Crimp the edge decoratively. Brush with a glaze made by beating the egg yolk with the frozen concentrate. Make several slits for steam vents. Bake for 10 minutes, then reduce the heat to 350° F. and continue to bake for 45 to 60 minutes.

Cool the pie on a wire rack. Serve warm or at room temperature.

Yield: 6 servings

Apple Pie "Plus"

The "plus" is a cheddar cheese topping, a counterpoint to the sweet apple flavor. Depending on the variety of apple, if you make 1/4-inch slices they will still be slightly crisp after baking. To add a chewy texture, as well as more flavor, use unpeeled apples. The pie shell is baked twice, a technique you can try in any pie if you want to be sure the crust stays crisp.

PIE

9-inch pie shell, baked
  (pages 72 and 74)
5 to 6 cups tart apples,
  sliced 1/8-inch to 1/4-inch
  thick and halved crosswise
1/4 cup frozen apple juice
  concentrate, at room
  temperature
Grated rind of 1 lemon
1 teaspoon lemon juice
1 teaspoon cornstarch
1 teaspoon cinnamon
1/2 teaspoon nutmeg

TOPPING

1/2 cup unbleached all-
  purpose or whole wheat
  pastry flour
1/4 teaspoon nutmeg
1 cup (4 ounces) grated
  cheddar cheese
3 tablespoons unsweetened
  shredded coconut or
  shredded wheat cereal
1/4 cup butter or
  margarine, melted

Preheat the oven to 350° F. Prepare the pie shell and set aside.

To make the topping, toss the flour, nutmeg, cheese, and coconut with the melted butter. Set aside.

To make the filling, toss the apples with the apple juice concentrate, lemon rind, and lemon juice. Mix together the cornstarch, cinnamon, and nutmeg and stir gently into apples. Place in the pie shell and evenly sprinkle with the topping. Bake for 50 to 60 minutes.

Cool the pie on a wire rack. Serve warm or at room temperature.

Yield: 6 servings

Lattice-Top Mince Pie

The earliest mincemeat pies were filled with a generously spiced mixture of chopped fruits, suet, and meat. Today, mincemeat is known as mock mince or just plain mince, with meat and suet rarely included as ingredients. This winter pie uses dried fruits and carrots. A variation is given that uses fresh summer fruits (see below).

The filling can be prepared 1 day ahead. Refrigerate until needed, but bring to room temperature before using.

Pastry for 1 double-crusted
  9-inch or 10-inch pie
  (pages 72 and 75), chilled
1-1/2 cups grated carrots
1-1/2 cups raisins
3/4 cup frozen apple juice
  concentrate
1/4 cup water
3 tablespoons cornstarch
1 teaspoon cinnamon
1/2 teaspoon nutmeg
1/4 teaspoon ground cloves
1/4 teaspoon allspice
1/4 teaspoon salt
2 cups coarsely chopped
  tart green apples (peeling
  optional)
1 medium-size orange,
  including peel, seeded
  and chopped
3 tablespoons butter or
  margarine
1/3 cup frozen orange juice
  concentrate
1/2 cup grape juice
2 tablespoons cider vinegar
1 teaspoon rum or brandy
  extract (optional)
2/3 cup chopped walnuts

Roll out the larger half of the chilled dough and line a 9-inch pie plate, leaving a 1-inch overhang. Refrigerate while preparing the filling.

In a saucepan, mix together the carrots, raisins, apple juice concentrate, and water. Bring to a boil, reduce the heat, and simmer for 5 minutes, stirring frequently. Set aside.

In a small bowl, mix together the cornstarch, spices, and salt. Set aside.

Stir the apples, orange, butter, orange juice concentrate, grape juice, and vinegar into the carrot-raisin mixture. Mix in the cornstarch and spices. Cook over moderate heat, stirring constantly for 3 to 4 minutes, until thickened. Stir in the extract and nuts. Cool.

Preheat the oven to 375° F.

Spoon the cooled filling into the lined pie plate, mounding it slightly higher in the center. Roll out the remaining dough into a rectangle about 1/8 inch thick and 11 inches long. Trim the ragged edges. Using a pastry wheel or sharp knife, cut the rectangle into 10 lengthwise strips, each 1/2 inch wide. To form the lattice, lay 5 strips 1 inch apart across filling. Working from the center, interweave the remaining strips, one at a time, over and under the first strips. Trim the ends. Moisten the overhanging edge of the bottom crust and fold up over the ends of the strips. Flute the edge of the crust. Place the pie on a baking sheet and bake for 30 to 45 minutes or until bubbly.

Summer Fruit Mince Pie. Substitute 3 cups chopped nectarines or peeled peaches (fresh or unsweetened frozen and defrosted) for the carrots.

Yield: 6 servings

Four-Fruit Pie

The filling can be prepared 1 day ahead. Refrigerate until needed, but bring to room temperature before using.

Pastry for Double-Crust
  9-inch or 10-inch Yogurt
  Dough (page 72), chilled
1 1/4 cups dried apricots
1-1/4 cups pitted prunes
1 cup golden raisins
Apple juice
2 cups coarsely chopped
  tart green apples
1 tablespoon grated orange
  rind
1/3 cup orange juice
1/2 cup coarsely chopped
  walnuts
1 teaspoon cinnamon
2 tablespoons melted butter

Roll out the larger half of the chilled yogurt dough and line a 9-inch pie plate, leaving a 1-inch overhang. Refrigerate while you prepare the filling.

In a saucepan, combine the apricots, prunes, and raisins. Pour over enough apple juice to cover the fruit. Bring to a boil, reduce the heat, and simmer for 10 minutes, stirring occasionally. Drain the fruit, reserving the liquid for another use, and chop into coarse pieces. Combine with the apples, orange rind, orange juice, walnuts, cinnamon, and melted butter. Allow the mixture to cool.

Preheat the oven to 425° F.

Spoon the cooled filling into the lined pie plate, mounding it slightly higher in the center. Roll out the remaining dough into a rectangle about 1/8 inch thick and 11 inches long. Trim the ragged edges. Using a pastry wheel or sharp knife, cut the rectangle into 10 lengthwise strips, each 1/2 inch wide. To form the lattice, lay 5 strips 1 inch apart across filling. Working from the center, interweave the remaining strips, one at a time, over and under the first strips. Trim the ends. Moisten the overhanging edge of bottom crust and fold up over the ends of the strips. Flute the edge of the crust. Place the pie on a baking sheet. Bake for 10 minutes, then reduce the heat to 350°. Bake for another 20 to 30 minutes or until golden.

Cool the pie on a wire rack.

Yield: 6 servings

Glazed Cream Cheese Pie

Count on serving seconds of Glazed Cream Cheese Pie. It's a do-ahead dessert that can be served on your best china at an elegant dinner or on paper plates at a picnic. Decorate the top with a single fruit, or combine several fruits in a colorful pattern. Either way the sparkling fruit topping makes this a glamorous pie.

DATE CRUMB CRUST

3/4 cup finely ground dry
  bread crumbs
1/4 cup (2 ounces) finely
  chopped dates, well packed
2 tablespoons butter or
  margarine, melted
1 tablespoon frozen apple
  juice concentrate

FILLING

1/2 cup golden raisins
1/4 cup frozen apple juice
  concentrate, at room
  temperature
2 egg yolks
1/4 cup milk
1 teaspoon vanilla extract
2 tablespoons flour
8 ounces low-fat cream
  cheese, at room
  temperature
2 egg whites, at room
  temperature
1/8 teaspoon cream
  of tartar
1/8 teaspoon salt

To make the crust, lightly grease a 9-inch pie plate. Combine the crumbs, dates, and melted butter with a fork. Stir in the apple juice concentrate. Press the mixture into the bottom and up the sides of pie plate. Set aside.

Preheat the oven to 325° F.

To make the filling, puree the raisins and apple juice concentrate in a blender or food processor. Add the egg yolks, milk, vanilla, flour, and cream cheese. Blend until smooth.

Beat the egg whites until foamy. Add the cream of tartar and salt, continuing to beat until the whites are stiff but not dry. Gently fold into the cheese mixture. Pour into the prepared crust and bake for 40 to 45 minutes or until firm.

Cool the pie on a rack. Meanwhile prepare one or more fruit toppings.

Drain the fruit, reserving any juice. In a saucepan, combine the reserved juice with additional fruit juice to make 2/3 cup. Make a paste with the cornstarch and 2 tablespoons of the juice. Mix until smooth. Then stir into the juice in the saucepan, along with the orange rind. Slowly bring the mixture to a boil; boil for 1 minute, stirring constantly until thickened. Remove from the heat and fold in the drained fruit.

FRUIT TOPPING

2 cups fruit (blueberries, black cherries, sliced peaches, or crushed pineapple – fresh or unsweetened canned or frozen and defrosted)
Fruit juice (grape for dark fruits; apple or pineapple for light fruits)
1 tablespoon cornstarch
1 teaspoon grated orange rind

Cover the pie with the fruit topping and chill. Serve cold.

Yield: 6 servings

Fruit Pizza

The eye-dazzling effect of this pizza-like tart never ceases to thrill us. Depending on the fruits we choose, the pattern of the pizza is different every time.

CRUST

1/3 cup frozen apple juice concentrate
3 tablespoons frozen orange juice concentrate
2/3 cup golden raisins
5 tablespoons butter or margarine
1 teaspoon vanilla extract
1 cup unbleached all-purpose flour
1 cup whole wheat pastry flour
1 teaspoon baking powder
1/4 teaspoon salt
Ice water

Preheat the oven to 350° F. Lightly grease a 12-inch to 14-inch pizza or tart pan.

To make the crust, combine the apple juice and orange juice concentrates and raisins in a small saucepan. Simmer until the raisins are slightly softened, 2 to 3 minutes. Remove from the heat and stir in the butter and vanilla. Puree the mixture in a blender or food processor until thoroughly blended, then transfer to a bowl.

Stir together the flours, baking powder, and salt. Combine with the pureed raisin mixture, adding a little ice water, if necessary, to make the dough workable. Form into a pancake shape. Place in the center of the pan and press outward to evenly cover the surface. Form a rim at the edge. Bake for 12 to 15 minutes. Cool the pizza on a wire rack.

FILLING

6 ounces low-fat cream
  cheese, at room
  temperature
1 teaspoon grated lemon rind
2-1/2 teaspoons frozen
  apple juice concentrate, at
  room temperature
2-1/2 teaspoons frozen
  orange juice concentrate,
  at room temperature
Berry halves, orange
  sections, seedless grape
  halves, raspberries,
  blueberries or any other
  fruits in season, drained

GLAZE

1/2 cup apple juice
2 teaspoons cornstarch
2 teaspoons water

To make the filling, mash the cream cheese with lemon rind and fruit juice concentrates in a small bowl, beating until smooth. Spread evenly over the entire crust. Arrange any combination of fruits in a single layer over cream cheese.

To make the glaze, heat the apple juice in a small saucepan. Make a paste with the cornstarch and water and add to the apple juice. Bring slowly to a boil. Boil for 1 minute, stirring constantly until thickened and clear. Cool slightly and brush or spoon over the fruit. Chill until served.

Yield: 10 servings

Upside-Down Pear Tart

A cousin to the Pineapple Upside-Down Coffeecake, Upside-Down Pear Tart is also made in a skillet. After baking, the skillet is flipped onto a serving plate to reveal a lovely, circular pattern of glossy, caramel-colored pears.

Pastry for 10-inch pie shell
(pages 72 and 74)
6 large firm, ripe pears of
equal size (about 2-1/2
pounds), peeled (optional),
cored, and sliced into sixths
1-1/2 teaspoons grated
lemon rind
1 tablespoon lemon juice
1/2 teaspoon cinnamon
1/8 teaspoon cloves
1/4 cup butter or
margarine, melted
1/2 cup frozen apple juice
concentrate
1/3 cup orange juice

Prepare the dough for a 10-inch pie shell. Roll out the dough between sheets of waxed paper to form an 11-inch round. Refrigerate while preparing the filling.

Slice the pears into a bowl and toss with the lemon rind, lemon juice, cinnamon, and cloves. Arrange the pears in two slightly overlapping circles on the bottom of a greased 10-inch skillet (the skillet should be oven-proof and about 2 inches deep), keeping the pointed ends of the fruit toward the center.

In a small saucepan, combine the melted butter, apple juice concentrate, and orange juice. Cook over moderate heat until syrupy, 10 to 15 minutes. Pour the thickened juices evenly over the pears. Bring to a boil, then cover and reduce the heat. Simmer for 5 minutes. Uncover and remove from the heat.

Preheat the oven to 425° F.

Remove the top sheet of the waxed paper and invert the chilled dough over the pears, gently fitting it against the sides of the pan. Trim with a knife, leaving a 1/4-inch border. Using a fork, prick the dough and crimp the edge against the side of the pan. Bake the tart for 10 minutes. Reduce the heat to 375° and bake for 20 to 25 minutes more, or until the pastry is golden brown. Cool on a wire rack for 10 minutes.

To serve, release the sides of the tart with a knife and invert it onto a serving plate. Wait several minutes before removing the skillet. If some of the pears stick, gently lift them off with a spatula and rearrange them on top of the tart. If the tart has trouble releasing, place a saucepan containing a small amount of boiling water on the bottom of the inverted skillet to soften the syrup.

Spoon any remaining syrup over the pears. Serve while still warm.

Yield: 6 servings

Upside-down Apple Tart. Substitute 6 apples (peeling optional) sliced into eighths for the pears.

Anyfruit Tartlets

The tartlet is a miniature tart for individual servings. It can be rectangular, round, or made in small fluted tins or muffin pans. Consider preparing a double recipe of tartlet shells and keeping the extras on hand in the freezer for last minute preparations. For the filling, use such fruits as pineapple, peaches, cherries, berries, bananas, seedless grapes, kiwi fruit. Use unsweetened fruits. Peel, pit, slice, and drain as desired.

Pastry for tartlet shells
 (pages 73 and 75), chilled
1 egg white
1 teaspoon frozen apple
 juice concentrate, room
 temperature
Fruit
Orange Glaze (page 208) or
 Strawberry Glaze
 (page 208)

Preheat the oven to 400° F. Lightly grease 24 muffin cups or tartlet molds.

Form the chilled dough into 24 balls each about 1 inch in diameter. Press each ball into the bottom and up sides of the cups or molds. Brush with an egg wash made by beating the egg white with the apple juice concentrate. Bake for 15 to 20 minutes or until golden.

Cool for 5 minutes, then carefully remove the shells from the molds by inserting the tip of a sharp knife between the crust and the pan. Cool on a wire rack.

Fill the tartlet shells with the fruit, using one kind of fruit in each shell. Cover the fruit completely with one of the glazes. The orange glaze should be used over light fruits, such as pineapple, peaches, bananas, grapes, kiwi fruit. The strawberry glaze should be used over dark fruits, such as cherries and berries.

Yield: 24 tartlets

Prune Tart

This is a dessert of German origin taken from a handwritten recipe found tucked inside an old cookbook. Pastry is pressed into a pan, then filled with a cooked prune mixture, and baked. The crowning touch is a meringue cap topped with crunchy almonds.

PASTRY

4 tablespoons butter or
  margarine
1-1/2 cups unbleached
  all-purpose flour
1 egg, lightly beaten
Grated rind of 1 lemon
Frozen apple juice
  concentrate

FILLING

1-1/2 pounds pitted prunes
Water
Grated rind and juice of
  1 lemon

MERINGUE TOPPING

3 egg whites, at
  room temperature
1/4 teaspoon cream
  of tartar
1/8 teaspoon salt
1/3 cup unsweetened
  applesauce (see page 187)
Cinnamon
1 cup chopped almonds

Lightly grease and flour a 9-inch springform or pan with a removable bottom.

To make the pastry, cut the butter into the flour until it looks like coarse meal. Add the egg, lemon rind, and enough apple juice concentrate to hold the mixture together. Pat the dough into the pan. Press the dough up along the sides to form a rim about 1-1/2 inches tall.

To make the filling, place the prunes in a saucepan with enough water to cover and cook until soft. Drain well and chop fine. Add the lemon rind and juice. Allow the mixture to cool. Spoon into the unbaked pastry crust.

Preheat the oven to 350° F.

To make the meringue topping, beat the egg whites until foamy. Add the cream of tartar and salt and continue beating until stiff but not dry. Fold in the applesauce and 1/2 teaspoon cinnamon. Spread on top of the prune mixture. Sprinkle the almonds and a little more cinnamon over top. Bake for 45 to 55 minutes, or until the meringue is lightly browned.

Cool the tart in its pan on a wire rack. Serve it warm or at room temperature.

Yield: 8 servings

Pecan Tartlets

Pecan Tartlets are derived from the old-fashioned southern "tassies." They are likely to disappear fast.

CREAM CHEESE DOUGH

3 ounces low-fat cream cheese, at room temperature
1/2 cup butter or margarine, at room temperature
1 teaspoon frozen apple juice concentrate
1 cup unbleached all-purpose flour (or use half whole wheat pastry flour)
1 teaspoon grated orange rind

FILLING

1 egg
1 tablespoon unbleached all-purpose flour
1 teaspoon cinnamon
Pinch salt
1/3 cup frozen apple juice concentrate, at room temperature
1 teaspoon vanilla extract
1/2 cup chopped raisins
2/3 cup chopped pecans

Lightly grease 24 miniature muffin cups or mini-tartlet molds.

To make the dough, blend the cream cheese and butter together. Stir in the apple juice concentrate, flour, and orange rind. Gather the mixture into a ball. Flatten into a pancake; wrap and refrigerate while you prepare the filling.

To make the filling, beat together the egg, flour, cinnamon, and salt. Stir in the apple juice concentrate, vanilla, raisins, and pecans.

Preheat the oven to 350° F.

Shape the pastry into 24 balls. Press each ball into the bottom and up the sides of the muffin cups. Spoon a small amount of filling into each pastry shell. Bake for 25 to 30 minutes. Cool on wire racks for 5 minutes, then carefully remove the tartlets by inserting the tip of a sharp knife between the crust and the pan. Let the tartlets cool completely before serving.

Yield: 24 mini-tartlets

Yogurt Pie Dough

This is a rich, tender pastry that bakes to a golden brown.

1/3 cup butter or
  margarine, at room
  temperature
1/2 cup plain nonfat yogurt
  or low-fat sour cream
3/4 cup unbleached all-
  purpose flour
1/2 cup whole wheat pastry
  flour
1/4 teaspoon salt

In a large bowl, cream together the butter and yogurt. In another bowl, combine the flours and salt and stir into the butter mixture, 1/4 cup at a time, until well-combined. Add 1 to 2 tablespoons more flour if the dough is sticky. Gather the mixture together and flatten it into a thick pancake. Wrap and refrigerate for at least 20 minutes.

On a lightly floured board or between sheets of waxed paper, roll the chilled dough into a 12-inch circle. Fold the circle in half, lift it off the board, and lay the fold across the center of 9-inch or 10-inch pie plate. Unfold and ease dough loosely into place without stretching it. Trim the overhanging edge 1/2 inch larger than the outside rim of the plate. Fold it under, even with rim of the pie plate, and crimp or flute the edge. Chill the pie shell in the refrigerator for 15 minutes.

Then fill and bake in a recipe or bake unfilled. To bake unfilled, preheat the oven to 400° F. Prick the crust all over the bottom and sides with a fork. Bake for 15 to 20 minutes or until golden. Cool before adding a filling.

Yield: 9-inch or 10-inch pie shell

Double Crust Yogurt Dough

2/3 cup butter or
  margarine, at room
  temperature
1 cup plain nonfat yogurt
  or low-fat sour cream
1-1/2 cups unbleached
  white flour
1 cup whole wheat pastry
  flour
1/8 teaspoon salt

In a large bowl, cream together the butter and yogurt. In another bowl, combine the flours and salt and stir into the butter mixture, 1/4 cup at a time, until well-combined. Add 1 to 2 tablespoons more flour if the dough is sticky. Divide into 2 portions, one slightly larger than the other. Flatten each into a thick pancake. Wrap and refrigerate for several hours. Roll out to make 9-inch or 10-inch double-crusted pies or 24 tartlet shells.

To make a bottom crust, place the larger half of the

chilled dough on a floured board or between sheets of waxed paper and roll it into a 12-inch circle. Fold the circle in half, lift it off the board, and the lay the fold across the center of 9-inch or 10-inch pie plate. Unfold and ease dough loosely into place without stretching it. Trim the overhanging edge even with the rim of the pie plate. Fill the crust with the desired filling.

To make the top crust, roll out the remaining dough into an 11-inch circle. Moisten the edge of the bottom crust with water. Fold the dough circle in half, lift off the board, place it across the center of filled pie, and unfold. Trim the edge 1/2 inch larger than the pie plate and tuck the overhang under the edge of bottom crust. Crimp the edges together with a fork or make a fluted pattern with your fingers. Make several decorative slits into the top crust to allow steam to escape. Chill the pie in the refrigerator for 15 minutes. Bake as directed in the recipe used.

To make tartlet shells, form the chilled dough into two 12-inch cylinders and divide each cylinder into 12 pieces. Shape each piece into a ball. Press into greased muffin cups or roll into a 4-inch or 5-inch round on a floured board or between sheets of waxed paper. Fit each round into an individual tartlet pan. Fill and bake as desired.

To make prebaked tartlet shells, preheat the oven to 400° F. Fit the chilled dough pieces into the muffin cups, or roll out and fit into tartlet pans, or drape over the bottoms of inverted custard cups. Prick well with a fork. Bake for 15 minutes or until browned. Gently remove the shells to a wire rack to cool before filling.

Yield: Double crust for a 9-inch or 10-inch pie or 24 tartlet shells

Crisp Oil Pie Shell

Vegetable oil takes the place of dairy products as the shortening ingredient in this dough, giving a crisp, wheaty brown crust rather than a pliable, tender one. Roll out oil dough between sheets of waxed paper. The dough can be used for both pie crusts and tart shells.

3/4 cup whole wheat pastry
   flour
3/4 cup unbleached all-
   purpose flour
1/4 teaspoon cinnamon
1/8 teaspoon salt
6 tablespoons vegetable oil
3 to 4 tablespoons apple or
   orange juice

Sift together the flours, cinnamon, and salt into a large bowl. Add the oil all at once, tossing quickly with a fork until the mixture has the consistency of coarse meal. Add 3 tablespoons of the juice all at once, stirring lightly until just blended. Add a little more juice if the mixture is too dry. Form into a ball and flatten into a thick pancake. Roll out immediately.

To roll out, place the dough between sheets of waxed paper and roll it into a 12-inch circle. Remove the top sheet and invert the dough into a 9-inch or 10-inch pie plate. Gently peel off the remaining paper and ease the dough loosely into place without stretching it. Trim the overhanging edge 1/2 inch larger than the outside rim of the pie plate and tuck the overhang under the edge of crust. Crimp the edges together with a fork or make a fluted pattern with your fingers. Prick the bottom and sides with a fork. Chill in the refrigerator for 15 minutes.

Bake the pie shell as directed for the filling used. Or bake unfilled by preheating the oven to 400° F. Bake for 15 to 20 minutes.

Yield: 9-inch or 10-inch pie shell

Double Crust Oil Dough

1-1/2 cups whole wheat
  pastry flour
1-1/2 cups unbleached all-
  purpose flour
1/2 teaspoon cinnamon
1/4 teaspoon salt
3/4 cup vegetable oil
6 to 8 tablespoons apple or
  orange juice

Sift together the flours, cinnamon, and salt into a large bowl. Add the oil all at once, tossing quickly with a fork until the mixture has the consistency of coarse meal. Add 6 tablespoons of the juice all at once, stirring lightly until just blended. Add a little more juice if the mixture is too dry. Form into a ball and divide the dough into 2 portions, one slightly larger than the other. Flatten each into a thick pancake. Roll out immediately.

To roll out the bottom crust, place the larger half of the dough between sheets of waxed paper and roll it into a 12-inch circle. Remove the top sheet and invert the dough into a 9-inch or 10-inch pie plate. Gently peel off the remaining paper and ease the dough loosely into place without stretching it. Trim the overhanging edge even with the rim of the the pie plate. Fill the crust with the desired filling.

To roll out the top crust, place the remaining dough between two more sheets of waxed paper and roll it into an 11-inch circle. Remove the top sheet and invert the dough onto the filled pie. Trim the edge 1/2 inch larger than the pie plate and tuck the overhang under edge of bottom crust. Crimp the edges together with a fork or make a fluted pattern with fingers. Make several slits across the top of crust to allow steam to escape. Chill in the refrigerator for 15 minutes. Bake as directed in the recipe used.

To make tartlet shells, form the dough into two 12-inch cylinders and divide each cylinder into 12 pieces. Shape each piece into a ball. Press into greased muffin cups or roll into a 4-inch or 5-inch round between sheets of waxed paper. Fit each round into an individual tartlet pan. Fill and bake as desired.

To make prebaked tartlet shells, preheat the oven to 400° F. Fit the dough pieces into the muffin cups, or roll out and fit into tartlet pans, or drape over the bottoms of inverted custard cups. Prick well with a fork. Bake for 15 minutes or until browned. Gently remove the shells to a wire rack to cool before filling.

Yield: Double crust for 9-inch or 10-inch pie or 24 tartlet shells

Filled Pastries, Strudels, & Dessert Crêpes

These are impressive, eye-catching desserts. Filled pastries take time to make, but they are always greeted with great enthusiasm, as are strudels and crêpes.

A few different doughs are used in these pastries, some easier to handle than others. All will handle best if the ingredients are cold. Handle the dough as quickly as possible and use a light touch. The pastry improves in texture if it is allowed to rest before baking. If possible, chill the pastry for at least 30 minutes in the refrigerator after it is shaped.

The one thing that ruins a filled pastry is a soggy filling. If your fruit is especially juicy, be sure to drain it well before adding to the other filling ingredients.

Our strudel recipes call for tissue-like sheets of pastry called phyllo (phyllo is the Greek word for leaf). If your supermarket does not carry phyllo in its freezer or dairy section, look for it on the shelves of Greek, Armenian, or Italian groceries. It is packaged by the pound, about 16 sheets or leaves per package. Fresh phyllo is best as the frozen dough becomes slightly brittle. But take what you can get. Defrost phyllo in its package in the refrigerator the day before you plan to use it.

Phyllo is remarkably easy to use. If a sheet happens to tear while you are working with it, touch the tear with a drop of water and mend with a patch cut from another phyllo sheet.

Because it is very thin, phyllo dries out quickly. Have your fillings and all ingredients ready before you unwrap the dough. Work rapidly and keep unused sheets covered with plastic wrap as you work.

To reduce the amount of fat used when making strudel, coat each sheet of phyllo with butter-flavored cooking spray, or brush lightly with vegetable oil instead of melted butter. The pastry will be just as flaky when it is baked.

Leftover phyllo can be kept for several weeks in the

refrigerator if it is well wrapped. Or it can be frozen for up to a month.

Strudel can be prepared 1 day ahead, brushed with melted butter, and, when the butter is firm, wrapped and refrigerated until you are ready to bake it the following day. Unbaked strudel will keep in the freezer for 2 weeks.

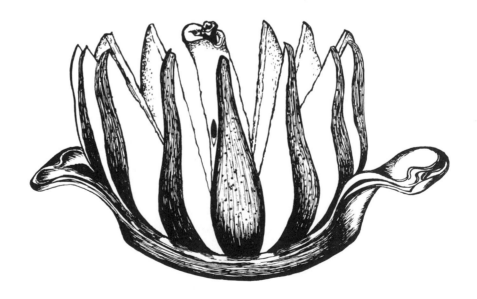

Prune Pockets

Although Prune Pockets are of Middle Eastern origin, their appearance brings to mind the tri-colored hats worn by the patriots of the American Revolution.

You will need to allow 2 hours for chilling the dough and cooling the filling. Both the filling and the dough can be prepared up to 2 days ahead.

DOUGH

3/4 cup butter or margarine, chilled
2 cups unbleached all-purpose flour (or use half whole wheat pastry flour
1 cup low-fat sour cream or plain nonfat yogurt
1 egg yolk
1 teaspoon grated lemon rind

FILLING

1-1/2 cups chopped prunes, well packed
1/4 cup chopped raisins
1 cup apple juice (or 1/4 cup frozen apple juice concentrate and 3/4 cup water)
1/2 cup toasted chopped almonds
2 teaspoons grated orange rind

EGG WASH

1 egg, beaten
1 teaspoon frozen apple juice concentrate, at room temperature

To make the dough, cut the butter into the flour until the texture resembles coarse cornmeal. Combine the sour cream, egg yolk, and lemon rind and blend into the flour mixture. Divide the dough into 3 parts, shaping each into a thick pancake. Wrap to prevent drying and refrigerate for several hours or overnight.

To make the filling, simmer the prunes and raisins in the apple juice for 10 to 15 minutes or until almost all of the liquid is absorbed. Add the almonds and orange rind. Set aside to cool.

On a lightly floured board, roll out one piece of dough at a time until it is a little less than 1/8 inch thick. Cut the dough into 3-inch rounds and place a teaspoon of filling in the center. Use a pastry brush or your fingertip to place a dot of water at the 12 o'clock, 4 o'clock, and 8 o'clock positions on each round. Bring the moistened areas together to form a three-pointed pocket or triangle. Pinch to seal, leaving a bit of filling visible at the corners. Place the pockets on 2 lightly greased cookie sheets. Brush with an egg wash made by beating the egg with the apple juice concentrate. Refrigerate until you are ready to bake.

Preheat the oven to 350° F.

Bake the pastries for 20 to 25 minutes or until lightly browned. Cool for 5 minutes on the cookie sheets before transferring the pastries to wire racks to cool completely.

Store leftover pastries in an airtight container in the refrigerator or freezer. Reheat Prune Pockets for about 5 minutes in a 300° F. oven.

Yield: 4 dozen

Apple Wrap-Ups

When you are in the mood to have fun with dough, to make tucks and pleats and a topknot of leaves, try these Apple Wrap-Ups. Wrap-ups are at their best when served right from the oven; later they become soggy.

Allow 30 minutes for the pastry to chill before baking.

PASTRY

3/4 cup unbleached all-
   purpose flour
1/2 cup whole wheat pastry
   flour
1/2 teaspoon ginger
1/2 teaspoon nutmeg
1/2 cup butter or margarine
1/2 cup small-curd low-fat
   cottage cheese

FILLING

1/4 cup raisins
1/4 cup (2 ounces) chopped
   dates, well packed
1/4 cup chopped walnuts
1 teaspoon cinnamon
6 small, tart apples (about
   3 inches in diameter),
   cored and peeled (optional)
1 egg
1 teaspoon frozen apple
   juice concentrate, at
   room temperature

To make the pastry, combine the flours and spices in a large bowl. With a pastry blender or 2 knives, cut in the butter until the mixture is coarse and crumbly. Stir in the cottage cheese with a fork, blending until the dough forms a ball. If the dough seems dry, add a few drops of ice water or apple juice, just enough to hold the dough together. Turn out onto a lightly floured board and knead for 1 minute. Form into a cylinder, wrap, and refrigerate for 30 minutes.

To make the filling, combine the raisins, dates, and chopped walnuts with the cinnamon. Fill the core of each apple with some of the filling. Set aside.

Cut the chilled pastry into 6 equal parts. On a lightly floured board, flatten each portion into a circle and roll out just large enough to enclose 1 apple (about 6 inches in diameter and not more than 1/8 inch thick). Set aside a few dough trimmings for decorating the tops. Lightly brush each pastry circle with an egg wash made by beating the egg with the apple juice concentrate and place an apple in the center of it. Pull the dough up around apples and pinch the edges to seal the seams. Patch any gaps. Cut out small leaf shapes and attach to the apples

with the egg wash. Place the Apple Wrap Ups in a lightly greased 12-inch by 9-inch baking pan and refrigerate for 30 minutes or longer.

Preheat the oven to 375° F.

Brush the top of the pastries with the egg wash and prick in several places to allow steam to escape. Bake for 25 minutes. Brush again with egg wash and reduce the oven temperature to 300°. Bake for another 15 to 20 minutes. Remove from the pan with a broad spatula. Serve hot.

Yield: 6 servings

Crispy Date Won Tons

A sheet of Oriental noodle dough is wrapped around a moist date filling. The ends are twisted and it's quickly deep-fried until the noodle is crisp and crunchy. Won tons freeze beautifully. Serve after an Indonesian dinner.

1 package commercial won ton wrappers (fresh or frozen and defrosted)
1 cup (8 ounces) finely chopped dates, well packed
1/2 cup finely chopped walnuts
2 teaspoons grated orange rind
1 to 2 tablespoons orange juice
2 to 3 cups peanut oil
Cinnamon

In a medium-size bowl, combine the dates, walnuts, and orange rind. Add just enough orange juice to bind the ingredients together.

Shape a tablespoon of filling into a cylinder 1 inch long. Place the cylinder diagonally across a won ton skin, just below the center. Moisten the lower corner of the wrapper with a drop of water. Fold the corner over the filling and tuck it underneath. Roll up to completely cover filling. Twist the ends in opposite directions.

Heat the oil in wok or deep skillet to 375° F. Deep-fry 8 to 10 won tons at a time, turning them occasionally. When they are golden and crisped, remove and drain on paper towels.

When the won tons are cool, sprinkle with cinnamon.

Store in an airtight container in the refrigerator or freezer. Reheat won tons for 5 minutes in a 300° F. oven.

Yield: 2 to 3 dozen

Baked Fruit-Filled Turnovers

These sweet Mexican turnovers are a favorite finger food at fiestas on both sides of the border. The dough can be made ahead, formed into rounds, layered between sheets of waxed paper and frozen until you get ready for the baking stage.

It's best if the turnovers can chill for at least 30 minutes before they go into the hot oven. It improves the texture of the pastry.

Double Crust Yogurt
  Dough (page 72)
2 cups chopped mixed
  fresh fruits (peaches,
  nectarines, apples, pears;
  peeled if desired)
2 tablespoons frozen apple
  juice concentrate
1/4 cup (2 ounces) chopped
  dates, well packed
1 egg white
1 teaspoon water
Ground nutmeg

Wrap the 2 flattened dough rounds and refrigerate them for several hours before rolling them out. Lightly grease 2 cookie sheets.

Combine the chopped fruit in a saucepan with the apple juice concentrate and dates. Simmer over low heat for 3 to 4 minutes, stirring constantly. Remove from the heat, spread out on a plate, and chill.

On a lightly floured board or between sheets of waxed paper, roll out the dough to a thickness of 1/8 inch. Cut out twelve 4-inch circles. Brush the dough circles with the egg white beaten with the water to help prevent sogginess.

Pour off and reserve any juices from the fruit. Spoon a tablespoon of the drained fruit in the center of each circle, leaving at least 1/2 inch of dough exposed. Sprinkle with nutmeg.

Fold the turnovers in half and press the edges together with the tines of a fork. Prick the tops with a fork. Transfer to the greased cookie sheets, pulling the ends together to form a crescent shape. Chill for 30 minutes.

Preheat the oven to 350° F.

Brush the chilled turnovers with some of the reserved fruit juice. Bake for 15 minutes. Brush again with the juice and continue to bake for 10 to 12 more minutes.

The turnovers are at their best when served at once. Store leftover turnovers in an airtight container in the refrigerator or freezer. Reheat them for 5 minutes in a 300° F. oven.

Yield: 1 dozen

Crescent Puffs

Many of the shaped pastries we know today originated long ago as symbolic offerings to the gods. This miniature version of the croissant may have been an ancient symbol for the moon. There are a few fillings to choose from: nut, cheese, and apricot or strawberry jam.

DOUGH

3 ounces low-fat cream cheese, at room temperature

1/2 cup butter or margarine, at room temperature

1 cup unbleached all-purpose flour

NUT FILLING

2/3 cup finely chopped walnuts

2/3 cup finely chopped raisins

1 tablespoon finely ground dry bread crumbs

1 teaspoon cinnamon

1 teaspoon grated lemon rind

1 teaspoon frozen apple juice concentrate, at room temperature

Milk

EGG WASH

1 egg white

1 teaspoon frozen apple juice concentrate, at room temperature

TOPPING

Ground nuts (optional)

To make the dough, blend together the cream cheese and butter. Stir in the flour. Form the dough into 2 balls. Wrap tightly and chill for 30 minutes or until firm.

To make the nut filling, combine the walnuts and raisins. Blend in the bread crumbs, cinnamon, grated lemon rind, and frozen apple juice concentrate. Add just enough milk to hold mixture together.

Preheat the oven to 350° F. Grease a cookie sheet.

On a lightly floured board, roll each ball of dough into a round about 9 inches in diameter. Cut into 12 wedges. Place a teaspoon of filling on the outer edge of each wedge. Roll up toward the center of circle to the point. Brush each crescent with an egg wash made by beating the egg white with the apple juice concentrate. Dip in ground nuts if desired. Place with the point side underneath on the greased cookie sheet. Bake for 20 minutes, or until lightly browned.

Cool the puffs for 5 minutes on the cookie sheet before transferring to wire racks to cool completely.

Store leftover pastries in an airtight container in the refrigerator or freezer. Reheat Crescent Puffs for about 5 minutes in a 300° F. oven.

Yield: 2 dozen

Cheese Filling. Process 1/2 pound farmer or dry cottage cheese in a food processor until smooth (or press through a sieve). Blend in 1 egg white, 1 tablespoon frozen orange juice concentrate, 1 tablespoon nonfat yogurt, 1/4 cup finely minced golden raisins, and 1/2 teaspoon cinnamon. Substitute for the nut filling.

Apricot Jam. Substitute Apricot Jam (page 203) for the nut filling.

Strawberry Jam. Substitute Strawberry Jam (page 203) for the nut filling.

Orange Custard Cream Puffs

A French invention, cream puff pastry magically expands when it is baked and becomes a hollow shell ready to receive a delectable filling. This may sound complicated, but in reality cream puffs require little effort.

There will be filling enough to fill only 6 of the 12 cream puff shells because the filling will not thicken properly in a larger quantity. You could cut back on the cream puff shell recipe, but since shells store so easily, we suggest making the entire recipe and storing the extra for a few days in the refrigerator or freezing them in an airtight container. Freshen stored shells in a 375° F. oven for 5 minutes.

CREAM PUFF SHELLS

1 cup apple juice (or 1/4 cup frozen apple juice concentrate and 3/4 cup water)
1/2 cup butter
1/8 teaspoon salt
1/2 cup unbleached all-purpose flour
1/2 cup whole wheat pastry flour
4 large eggs, at room temperature

To make the cream puff shells, preheat the oven to 400° F. Line a large cookie sheet with foil.

In a heavy saucepan, combine the apple juice, butter, and salt. Bring to a boil over medium heat. When the liquid is boiling and the butter melted, pour in the flour all at once. Beat vigorously with a wooden spoon until blended. When the mixture pulls away from the sides of the pan and forms a ball, remove from the heat and set aside for 5 minutes, stirring occasionally to hasten the cooling process.

Be sure the eggs are at room temperature. Make a well in the center of cooled dough and blend in one egg at a time, beating thoroughly after each addition until the dough becomes smooth. Drop by rounded tablespoonfuls onto the lined baking sheet. Make 12 mounds of pastry, each 2 inches in diameter at the base, tapering it to a 1-inch peak at the top. (Use your fingers!) Leave 2 inches between mounds to permit spreading. (If you have a pastry bag, squeeze out the dough through a #7 or #8 plain tube.)

ORANGE CUSTARD FILLING

1-3/4 cups low-fat milk
3 tablespoons cornstarch
2 teaspoons unbleached all-purpose flour
1/8 teaspoon salt
1/8 teaspoon salt
1/4 cup frozen apple juice concentrate, at room temperature
2 tablespoons frozen orange juice concentrate, at room temperature
3 egg yolks
1 tablespoon grated orange rind
1 teaspoon vanilla extract
2 oranges, peeled, segmented, and cut into chunks

Bake the puffs for 15 minutes, being careful not to open oven door. Reduce the oven temperature to 300° and bake an additional 15 to 20 minutes. When the puffs are golden brown and sound hollow when tapped on the bottom, turn off the heat. Prick each puff with the tip of a sharp knife to release any steam trapped inside. Leave them in the oven with a partially open oven door for another 20 to 30 minutes.

Meanwhile, prepare the filling. In a heavy-bottomed saucepan, heat the milk until warmed. Mix the cornstarch, flour, and salt in a bowl. Add the milk slowly to the cornstarch mixture, stirring until smooth. Return the mixture to the saucepan and bring to a boil. Boil for 1 minute, stirring constantly until thickened. Remove from the heat and stir in the apple juice and orange juice concentrates.

With a fork, lightly beat the egg yolks. Stir 3 tablespoons of the hot milk mixture into the beaten egg yolks, then gradually stir the yolks into the remaining hot milk in the saucepan. Cook over low heat, stirring constantly until thickened, about 2 minutes. Remove from the heat and stir in the orange rind and vanilla. Transfer to a bowl. Cover the surface of the filling with plastic wrap to prevent a skin from forming and refrigerate until needed.

Fill the cream puff shells just before serving. To fill, use a sharp knife to slice the tops off 6 shells. Discard any doughy filaments inside. Drain the orange chunks and fold them into the filling. Put a tablespoon of filling inside each shell and replace its top. Serve immediately.

Yield: 6 filled cream puffs (plus 6 cream puff shells)

Fresh Apple Strudel

What could be more tempting than a slice of warm apple strudel, with its cinnamon-laced apples and crackling thin crust?

FILLING

3 apples, chopped
2 teaspoons grated lemon rind
1 tablespoon lemon juice
1/2 cup unsweetened canned crushed pineapple, well drained
1/2 cup dried currants
1/2 cup golden raisins
2/3 cup chopped walnuts
1 teaspoon cinnamon
2 tablespoons frozen apple juice concentrate, at room temperature
Finely ground dry bread crumbs

NUT-CRUMB MIXTURE

1 cup ground nuts
1/2 cup finely ground dry bread crumbs
2 teaspoons cinnamon

PASTRY

10 leaves phyllo dough
1/3 to 1/2 cup butter or margarine, melted

To make the filling, toss the apples with the lemon rind and lemon juice. Add the pineapple, currants, raisins, walnuts, cinnamon, and apple juice concentrate. Stir in enough bread crumbs to hold the mixture together and absorb the juices. The filling can be prepared 1 day ahead. Drain off any excess liquid before filling the strudel.

To make the nut-crumb mixture, combine the nuts, bread crumbs, and cinnamon. Set aside.

Preheat the oven to 350° F.

Place a damp tea towel on a work surface and cover it with waxed paper. Unwrap the phyllo dough and place 5 leaves on the waxed paper. (Keep the remaining leaves wrapped and return them to the refrigerator.) Fold the leaves together like a closed book and open to the first page. Brush it with melted butter and sprinkle with 1 tablespoon of the crumb mixture. Turn to the next page and repeat the butter and crumb process. Continue until you come to the center, but do not butter the center leaf yet. Close the book and turn it over. Starting from the back, repeat the process with butter and crumbs until you come to the center again. Brush the open center with butter and add a few more crumbs. Sprinkle a thick row of the crumb mixture along bottom edge of dough. Then carefully spoon half of the filling in a lengthwise strip next to the crumbs. Fold the bottom edge of the phyllo over the filling. Turn in the left and right sides and roll up the dough lengthwise, jelly-roll fashion, using the towel and waxed paper to help. Place seam-side down on a greased cookie sheet. Brush the surface of roll with melted butter.

Repeat the procedure using 5 more leaves of phyllo and the remaining filling. Place on a second greased cookie sheet.

Bake for 20 minutes, then remove from the oven and brush again with melted butter. To make slicing easier, cut diagonally halfway through the dough at 1-1/2-inch intervals. Return the strudel to the oven and bake for 20 additional minutes, or until golden brown and crisp.

Serve warm or at room temperature. Store leftover strudel in an airtight container in the refrigerator or freezer. Reheat strudel directly out of the freezer for about 5 or 10 minutes in a 300° F. oven.

Yield: 2 strudel rolls of 8 slices each

Pear Strudel. Substitute 3 pears for the apples.

Cherry Strudel

You can expect a pause in the conversation when hot cherry strudel emerges from the oven, and those plump sweet cherries are revealed with the first slice.

FILLING

6 cups (about 2 pounds) pitted black cherries (fresh or unsweetened canned or frozen and defrosted)
6 tablespoons frozen apple juice concentrate, at room temperature
1 tablespoon grated lemon rind
1/2 teaspoon almond extract
2-1/2 teaspoons cornstarch
2 teaspoons frozen apple juice concentrate at room temperature

NUT-CRUMB MIXTURE

1 cup ground nuts
1/2 cup finely ground dry bread crumbs
2 teaspoons cinnamon

PASTRY

10 leaves phyllo dough
1/3 to 1/2 cup butter or margarine, melted

In a saucepan, combine the cherries, 6 tablespoons apple juice concentrate, and lemon rind. Cover and simmer over low heat for 2 to 3 minutes. Add the almond extract and cornstarch dissolved in the remaining 2 teaspoons apple juice concentrate. Bring to a boil, stirring until thickened. If the mixture is too liquid, add another 1/2 teaspoon dissolved cornstarch. Set aside to cool. The filling can be prepared 1 day ahead. Drain off any excess liquid before filling the strudel.

Combine the nuts, bread crumbs, and cinnamon. Set aside.

Preheat the oven to 350° F.

Place a damp tea towel on a work surface and cover it with waxed paper. Unwrap the phyllo dough and place 5 leaves on the waxed paper. (Keep the remaining leaves wrapped and return them to the refrigerator.) Fold the leaves together like a closed book and open to the first page. Brush it with melted butter and sprinkle with 1 tablespoon of the crumb mixture. Turn to the next page and repeat the butter and crumb process. Continue until you come to the center, but do not butter the center leaf yet. Close the book and turn it over. Starting from the back, repeat the process with butter and crumbs until you come to the center again. Brush the open center with butter and add a few more crumbs. Sprinkle a thick row of crumb mixture along the bottom edge of the dough, then carefully spoon half of the filling in a lengthwise strip next to the crumbs. Fold the bottom edge of the phyllo over the filling. Turn in left and right sides and roll up the dough lengthwise, jelly-roll fashion, using the towel and waxed paper to help. Place seam-side down on a greased cookie sheet. Brush the surface of the roll with melted butter.

Repeat the procedure using 5 more leaves of phyllo and the remaining filling and nut-crumb mixture.

Bake for 20 minutes, then remove from the oven and brush again with melted butter. To make slicing easier, cut diagonally halfway through the dough at 1-1/2-inch intervals. Return the strudel to the oven and bake for 20 additional minutes, or until golden brown and crisp.

Serve warm or at room temperature. Store leftover strudel in an airtight container in the refrigerator or freezer. Reheat the strudel directly out of the freezer for about 5 or 10 minutes in a 300° F. oven.

Yield: 2 strudel rolls of 8 slices each

Dried Fruit Strudel

A yogurt dough gives this strudel a soft, tender texture in contrast to the strudels made with flaky phyllo dough. You will need to allow 2 hours for the yogurt dough to chill. Alternatively, the dough can be made days ahead or frozen. The filling can be made 1 day ahead. Substitute other dried fruits, such as figs, pears, peaches, or nectarines, depending on your mood.

YOGURT DOUGH

3/4 cup butter or margarine, at room temperature
1 cup plain nonfat yogurt
1-1/2 cups unbleached all-purpose flour
1 cup whole wheat pastry flour
1/4 teaspoon salt

FILLING

1 cup chopped dried apricots
1 cup (8 ounces) chopped dates, well packed
1 cup raisins
1/2 cup unsweetened crushed pineapple, drained (reserve the juice)
Unsweetened fruit juice
1 tablespoon lemon juice
1 tablespoon grated lemon rind
2 teaspoons cinnamon
1 cup toasted slivered almonds or 1/2 cup unsweetened shredded coconut and 1/2 cup toasted sunflower seeds

EGG WASH

1 egg white
1 teaspoon frozen apple juice concentrate, at room temperature

In a large bowl, cream together the butter and yogurt. In another bowl, combine the flours and salt and stir into the butter mixture, 1/4 cup at a time, until well-combined. Add 1 to 2 tablespoons more flour if the dough is sticky. Divide into 2 portions and flatten each into a thick pancake. Wrap and refrigerate for 2 hours or overnight.

In a small saucepan, combine the apricots, dates, raisins, and pineapple. Measure the reserved pineapple juice and add enough additional fruit juice to make 3/4 cup. Stir into the fruit, along with the lemon juice, lemon rind, and cinnamon. Cook over moderate heat for 4 to 5 minutes, or until most of the liquid is absorbed. Stir in the almonds or coconut and sunflower seeds. Let the mixture cool. Drain off any excess liquid before filling the strudel.

Preheat the oven to 350° F.

Remove 1 piece of yogurt dough from the refrigerator. Roll out on a lightly floured board or between sheets of waxed paper into a rectangle 6 inches by 18 inches. Spread half of the filling over the dough, keeping it 1/2 inch from the edges. Roll up the dough lengthwise and fit the strudel on a lightly greased cookie sheet, curving it if necessary to fit. Repeat the procedure with the second piece of pastry.

Brush the strudel rolls with an egg wash made by beating the egg white with the apple juice concentrate. Place in the preheated oven. Remove after 20 minutes and using scissors, cut partly through into 1-inch slices. Brush with the remaining egg wash. Sprinkle with cinnamon. Bake an additional 15 minutes or until golden brown. Remove from the oven and cut the slices through with a sharp knife.

Cinnamon

Serve warm or at room temperature. Store leftover strudel in an airtight container in the refrigerator or freezer. Reheat strudel directly out of the freezer for 5 to 10 minutes in a 300° F. oven.

Yield: 2 strudel rolls of 16 slices each

Cheese Strudel

Three cheeses are blended to make a creamy, light filling that hints of sweetness and spice.

FILLING

1/2 cup golden raisins
1/4 cup frozen apple juice
   concentrate, at room
   temperature
4 ounces hoop or farmer
   cheese
4 ounces low-fat cream
   cheese
8 ounces ricotta cheese
1 egg
1/2 teaspoon cinnamon
2 tablespoons unbleached
   all-purpose flour
1/8 teaspoon salt
1 teaspoon grated lemon rind

PASTRY AND BREAD CRUMBS

10 leaves of phyllo dough
1/3 to 1/2 cup butter or
   margarine, melted
1-1/4 cups finely ground dry
   bread crumbs

In a blender or food processor, puree the raisins and apple juice concentrate. Transfer to a bowl and set aside.

Process the hoop or farmer cheese in a food processor or press through a food mill or strainer. When the mixture is smooth, blend in the cream cheese and ricotta cheese. Combine with the pureed raisin mixture and add the egg, cinnamon, flour, salt, and lemon rind. Mix thoroughly. This filling can be prepared 1 day ahead and refrigerated.

Preheat the oven to 350° F.

Place a damp tea towel on a work surface and cover it with waxed paper. Unwrap the phyllo dough and place 5 leaves on the waxed paper. (Keep the remaining leaves wrapped and return them to the refrigerator.) Fold the leaves together like a closed book and open to the first page. Brush it with melted butter and sprinkle with 1 tablespoon bread crumbs. Turn to the next page and repeat the butter and crumb process. Continue until you come to the center, but do not butter the center leaf yet. Close the book and turn it over. Starting from the back, repeat the process with butter and crumbs until you come to the center again. Brush the open center with butter and add a few more crumbs. Starting 2 inches from the bottom edge, carefully spoon one-half of the filling in a lengthwise strip. Fold the bottom edge of phyllo over filling. Turn in the left and right sides and roll up dough lengthwise, jelly-roll fashion, using the towel and waxed paper to help. Place seam-side down on a greased cookie sheet. Brush the surface of the roll with melted butter.

Repeat the procedure using 5 more leaves of phyllo and the remaining filling. Place on a second greased cookie sheet.

Bake for 20 minutes, then remove from oven and brush again with melted butter. To make slicing easier, cut diagonally halfway through dough at 1-1/2-inch intervals.

Return the strudel to the oven and bake for 20 additional minutes or until golden brown and crisp.

Serve warm or at room temperature. Store leftover strudel in an airtight container in the refrigerator or freezer. Reheat strudel directly out of the freezer for about 5 or 10 minutes in a 300° F. oven.

Yield: 2 strudel rolls of 8 slices each

Basic Crêpes

To make crêpes, you will need a 6-inch crêpe or omelet pan or heavy-bottomed skillet with sloping sides. A nonstick surface works very well. A variation given below uses an 8-inch pan.

2 eggs
1 cup low-fat or whole milk
1/4 cup water
1 cup unbleached all-
    purpose or whole wheat
    pastry flour
1/8 teaspoon salt
1 tablespoon vegetable oil
Butter, margarine, or oil for
    coating pan

In a blender or bowl, combine all ingredients, except the butter or oil for coating the pan. Blend for 1 minute or beat by hand or with an electric mixer until smooth, scraping down the sides as needed. Cover and refrigerate the batter for at least 2 hours before making the crêpes. If the batter is thicker than cream after it has rested, thin it with a little more liquid.

Set the pan over moderate heat and when it is hot, grease it until it is well coated. Pour 2 to 3 tablespoons of batter into the pan and quickly tilt it in a circular motion until the batter is spread evenly over the surface. Note: If you use whole wheat pastry flour, stir as you pour out the batter each time to keep the bran from settling to the bottom of the batter.

Cook the crêpe for 1 minute or until slightly browned, then turn it and lightly brown the other side for about 30 seconds. Do not overcook. An overbrowned crêpe is difficult to roll. Remove the crêpe from the pan and lay it flat on a damp tea towel to cool.

Continue making crêpes until the batter is gone, keeping the pan well greased as needed. If the batter thickens, add a little water.

If you are making them ahead of time, separate the cooled crêpes with waxed paper, wrap the stack tightly, and refrigerate for up to 3 days. If you want to keep the crêpes longer, freeze them in small stacks wrapped in foil. To defrost, partially open the foil package and place it in the refrigerator overnight. To defrost more quickly, use a microwave (remove the foil wrapper) or heat the opened package in a 300° F. oven for 15 minutes. Crêpes are less likely to tear if you bring them to room temperature before you fill them.

Once you have filled the crêpes, heat for 15 minutes in the oven, then serve. Or fill the crêpes at the table.

Have the crêpes at room temperature and the filling either heated or at room temperature.

Yield: 18 to 22 crêpes

8-inch Crêpes. You will need an 8-inch crêpe or omelet pan or skillet with sloping sides. Follow the above procedures, pouring 1/4 cup of the batter into the pan for each crêpe. Yield: 8 to 10 crêpes.

Blueberry Crêpes

Blueberry crêpes are a favorite with kids. They love to smile and show off their blueberry teeth. As a variation, substitute any dark berry such as loganberry, ollalie berry, or blackberry. Serve the crêpes topped with plain nonfat yogurt or low-fat sour cream.

Twelve 5-inch or 6-inch
  crêpes (pages 96-98)
2-1/2 cups (12 ounces)
  unsweetened blueberries
  (fresh or frozen)
1/4 cup unsweetened grape
  juice
2 tablespoons frozen apple
  juice concentrate
2 teaspoons grated lemon
  rind
1/2 teaspoon cinnamon
2 teaspoons cornstarch
2 teaspoons water
2 teaspoons butter or
  margarine, melted

Prepare the crêpes and set aside to be filled.

Preheat the oven to 375° F. Lightly grease a 13-inch by 9-inch baking dish.

Rinse fresh blueberries and drain. (Defrost and drain frozen blueberries.)

In a saucepan, combine the grape juice, apple juice concentrate, lemon rind, and cinnamon. Simmer for 1 minute, then add the cornstarch dissolved in the water. Bring to a boil. Boil for 1 minute, stirring until thickened. Remove from heat and combine with the blueberries.

Put 2 tablespoons of the blueberry filling down the center of each crêpe. Roll up and place seam-side down in dish. Brush the crêpes with melted butter and heat in the oven for 15 minutes. Serve while still hot or warm.

Yield: 6 servings

Skinny Crêpes

Spread a heaping tablespoon of Pineapple-Apricot Marmalade (page 204) down the center of each crêpe and pop them in the oven for an elegant, last-minute dessert.

For these crêpes, you will need a 6-inch crêpe or omelet pan or nonstick skillet. For best results, spray the pan with a nonstick cooking spray since the batter has very little oil in it.

3 egg whites
1 cup lowfat milk
2 tablespoons nonfat dry milk powder
2 tablespoons apple juice (or 1 tablespoon water and 1 tablespoon frozen apple juice concentrate)
2 teaspoons vegetable oil
2 teaspoons grated orange or lemon rind (optional)
1 cup unbleached all-purpose flour
Pinch salt
Vegetable cooking spray

In a blender, combine all the ingredients and blend until thoroughly mixed. Scrape down any flour from the sides of the blender and blend once again.

Allow the batter to stand for at least 2 hours before using (or refrigerate for 2 to 3 days).

Coat the pan with cooking spray and set it over moderate heat. When it is hot, pour a small amount (about 1/8 cup) of batter into the pan and quickly tilt it in a circular motion until the batter is spread evenly over the surface. Cook the crêpe for 1 minute or until slightly browned, then turn it and lightly brown the other side for about 30 seconds. Remove the crêpe from the pan and lay it flat on a damp tea towel to cool.

Continue making crêpes, using additional vegetable spray as needed to prevent sticking. If the batter becomes too thick, add a little water.

Stack cooled crêpes between layers of waxed paper and store tightly covered in the refrigerator or freeze until needed. (See detailed storage suggestions in Basic Crêpes, page 96.)

Yield: 16 crêpes

Apple Crêpes

These luscious crêpes are filled with Golden Delicious apples sautéed with butter, raisins, and aromatic spices until lightly caramelized. The filling can be made 1 day ahead – or make a double recipe and store half in the freezer for a future day when there's no time to make a special dessert.

Twelve 6-inch crêpes
   (pages 96-98)
8 large Golden Delicious
   apples (or other apples
   that hold their shape
   while cooking)
Lemon juice
2 tablespoons butter or
   margarine
3 tablespoons frozen apple
   juice concentrate
3 tablespoons frozen orange
   juice concentrate
1/2 cup dried currants or
   raisins
2 teaspoons grated lemon
   rind
1-1/2 teaspoons cinnamon
1/3 cup chopped almonds
2 teaspoons butter or
   margarine, melted

Prepare the crêpes and set aside to be filled.

Lightly grease a 13-inch by 9-inch baking pan.

Peel the apples if desired, core, and cut into 1/4-inch slices. Sprinkle immediately with lemon juice to prevent discoloring. Heat the butter in a large skillet; add the apples and stir over medium heat for 2 minutes. Stir in the apple juice concentrate, orange juice concentrate, currants, lemon rind, cinnamon, and almonds. Simmer, covered, until the apples are softened, about 3 minutes. Uncover and cook until most of the liquid is absorbed. Cool.

Preheat the oven to 375° F.

Put 2 tablespoons of the apple filling down the center of each crêpe. Roll up and place seam-side down in the baking dish. Brush the crêpes with the melted butter and bake for 15 minutes. Serve while still hot or warm.

Yield: 6 servings

Black Cherry Crêpes

Unsweetened sliced peaches, pears, or apricots can be substituted for black cherries.

Twelve 6-inch crêpes
  (pages 96-98)
2-1/2 cups (12 ounces) pitted
  black cherries (fresh or
  unsweetened canned or
  frozen and defrosted)
2 tablespoons frozen apple
  juice concentrate
1/4 cup orange juice
1 tablespoon grated orange
  rind
1/2 teaspoon cinnamon
2 teaspoons cornstarch
1 tablespoon orange juice
2 teaspoons butter or
  margarine, melted
Sliced almonds

Prepare the crêpes and set aside to be filled.

Preheat the oven to 375° F. Lightly grease a 13-inch by 9-inch baking dish.

Drain the cherries of any excess liquid. Place them in a saucepan with the apple juice concentrate, 1/4 cup orange juice, orange rind, and cinnamon. Cover and simmer over low heat until the cherries are heated through. (Fresh cherries will need to cook for 3 to 4 minutes. Add the cornstarch dissolved in the remaining 1 tablespoon orange juice. Bring to a boil. Boil for 1 minute, stirring gently, until the sauce is thickened.

Put 2 tablespoons of the filling down the center of each crêpe. Roll up and place seam-side down in the baking dish. Brush the crêpes with melted butter and sprinkle with the sliced almonds. Bake for 15 minutes. Serve while still hot or warm.

Yield: 6 servings

Fresh Fruit Crêpes

If you have a package of crêpes waiting in the freezer, then all it takes is fresh fruit or a basket of berries to serve a fancy dessert at a moment's notice. No baking, just fill the crêpes with fruit, roll them up, and serve for luncheon, Sunday night supper, or for lap food where nothing but a fork is needed.

12 six-inch crêpes
(pages 96-97)
4 large ripe bananas
2 tablespoons milk
2 teaspoons frozen apple
juice concentrate, at room
temperature
1 tablespoon grated orange
rind
2-1/2 cups peaches and
pears or other seasonal
fruits (fresh or
(unsweetened canned or
frozen and defrosted)
3 tablespoons orange juice
Strawberry Sauce (page 204)

Prepare the crêpes and set aside to be filled.

Mash the bananas with the milk, apple juice concentrate, and orange rind. Spread a little of the mixture on each crêpe.

Peel, seed, and dice the fruits. Sprinkle with orange juice. Spoon some of the fruit mixture on each banana-covered crêpe. Roll up and place seam-side down on individual plates. Serve with Strawberry Sauce.

Yield: 6 servings

Many-Layered Crêpe Cake

A unique dessert in which crêpes are layered with cinnamon-spiced apples and toasted almonds and stacked into a cake. The preparation can be done a day ahead. Bring it to room temperature before baking. Serve topped with the Light Milk Whip (page 210).

Six 8-inch crêpes (page 97)
12 large Golden Delicious
  or other apples that will
  hold their shape while
  cooking
Lemon juice
3 tablespoons butter or
  margarine
1/3 cup frozen apple juice
  concentrate
1/3 cup orange juice
2 tablespoons minced dried
  apricots
2 teaspoons cinnamon
1/2 cup toasted sliced
  almonds
1 teaspoon melted butter
1 teaspoon frozen apple
  juice concentrate, at room
  temperature

Lightly grease a 9-inch or 10-inch pie plate or round baking dish.

Peel the apples if you like, then core and cut them into 1/4-inch slices. Sprinkle immediately with lemon juice to prevent discoloring. Heat the butter in a large skillet; add the apples and stir over medium heat for 2 minutes. Stir in the 1/3 cup apple juice concentrate, orange juice, apricots, and cinnamon. Cover and simmer until the apples are slightly softened, about 3 minutes. Uncover and cook until most of the liquid is absorbed.

Preheat the oven to 375° F.

Place one crêpe on the bottom of the pie plate; cover with a portion of the apples and sprinkle with a few almonds. Cover with another crêpe, pressing down on the center to spread the apples out to the edge. Continue layering with the crêpes, apples, and almonds, ending with enough apple mixture to cover the top. Brush the top with a glaze made by combining the melted butter with the remaining 1 teaspoon apple juice concentrate.

Bake for 15 minutes or until the apple topping has browned. If it hasn't browned, place the cake under broiler for several minutes.

Cut into wedges and serve while still hot or warm.

Yield: 6 servings

Cookies & more Cookies!

C risp and golden, soft and chewy, large or small, there is a cookie here to match your desires. If you are in a chocolate mood, try the Cocoa-Orange Macaroons. Or pack Apple-Fig Newtons into lunch bags. Fill the cookie jar with Peanut, Apple, 'n' Raisin Cookies for the after-school snacking crowd. All are great washed down with cold milk. Cheesecake Cookies make elegant, bite-sized treats for tea and Pecan Bark, with its yeasty, nut-laden flavor, asks for a freshly brewed cup of hot coffee.

Children love to take part in cookie baking. Pear Giants are especially fun to make, as are cookies that are rolled and then cut into fancy shapes, such as the Gingersnaps with a Bite and the Anise Seed Cut-Outs. While they participate in the making of virtuous desserts, children will be training their palates to prefer the sweetness that comes from wholesome, nourishing ingredients. They will be cultivating an awareness of healthful choices about desserts.

For an evenly baked cookie, use unrimmed baking sheets. Heavy gauge metal is best as it won't warp when heated. If your oven tends to overbrown the bottoms of cookies, try baking them on 2 sheets, one inside the other. When you place several sheets in the oven at once, stagger their positions so heat can circulate evenly. Staggering is a good way to compensate for oven hot spots. When re-using sheets, let them cool first.

When it comes to timing, cookies can be deceiving. Cookies are often disarmingly soft and limp when they are first removed from their baking sheets; however, they firm up beautifully as they cool. If you have let the cookies bake the maximum time called for by the recipe, it is better to trust that they are done, rather than return them to the oven and have overbaked cookies as a result.

It is important to slip the cookies onto wire racks

promptly so air can circulate around them. As long as cookies are in contact with the hot metal, they will continue to bake. Wait until the cookies are thoroughly cooled before overlapping or stacking them. Otherwise they will hold steam and become soggy.

Many cookies are at their best right out of the oven. If you get in the habit of preparing cookie dough in advance and freezing it (for up to 3 months), you need only to schedule thawing time to have the aroma of cookies baking.

Because virtuous dessert cookies are made without refined sugar or any other preservative, they need to be kept well-wrapped in the refrigerator. Store crisp cookies separately from moist, cakey cookies. When wrapped in airtight packaging, cookies can be frozen for up to 9 months. To re-crisp cookies, place them in a preheated 300° F. oven for 2 or 3 minutes.

Peanut, Apple, and Raisin Cookies

A great after-school or lunch box treat. The combination of nonfat milk, whole wheat flour, and nuts give these cookies a real protein boost.

1/2 cup whole wheat pastry flour
1/2 cup nonfat dry milk powder
1 teaspoon baking powder
1 teaspoon cinnamon
1 teaspoon nutmeg
1/4 teaspoon cloves
1/8 teaspoon salt (omit if peanuts or peanut butter are salted)
1/2 cup rolled oats (noninstant)
3/4 cup raisins
1/2 cup chopped dried apple or 3/4 cup grated raw apple
1/2 cup coarsely chopped peanuts
1/2 cup (4 ounces) coarsely chopped dates, well packed
1/3 cup frozen apple juice concentrate, at room temperature
1/4 cup vegetable oil
2 eggs
3/4 cup chunky peanut butter

Preheat the oven to 325° F. Lightly grease 2 cookie sheets.

In a large bowl, sift together the flour, milk powder, baking powder, cinnamon, nutmeg, cloves, and salt. Stir in the oats, raisins, dried or fresh apple, and peanuts, mixing until evenly distributed.

In a blender or food processor, puree the dates and apple juice concentrate. Blend in the oil, eggs, and peanut butter until just combined. Mix the date mixture with the dry ingredients, stirring to blend.

Drop by the teaspoon onto the cookie sheets. Press with a wet spoon or spatula to flatten. Bake for 15 to 20 minutes or until browned. Let the cookies cool briefly before removing them to wire racks to cool completely.

Yield: 5 dozen cookies

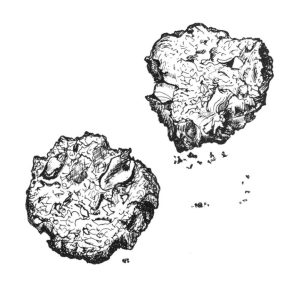

Gingerhots

The pungent flavor of freshly grated ginger and the crunch of sesame seeds give Gingerhots an unexpected taste and texture.

1-1/2 cups unbleached all-purpose flour or whole wheat pastry flour
1/4 teaspoon baking powder
1/4 teaspoon salt
1-1/2 teaspoons ground ginger
1/3 cup finely chopped golden raisins
1/3 cup (2-1/2 ounces) finely chopped dates, well packed
1/2 cup butter or margarine, at room temperature
1/2 cup frozen apple juice concentrate, at room temperature
1 teaspoon vanilla extract
1 tablespoon grated ginger root, firmly packed, or 2 to 2-1/2 teaspoons ground ginger
1/3 cup toasted sesame seeds
3 to 4 tablespoons untoasted sesame seeds

In a large bowl, sift together the flour, baking powder, salt, and 1-1/2 teaspoons ground ginger. Stir in the raisins and dates, mixing until evenly distributed.

In another bowl, combine the butter with the apple juice concentrate, vanilla, grated ginger root, and toasted sesame seeds. Work together with a fork.

Combine with the dry ingredients and blend. If the dough is too sticky to handle, chill until firm.

Preheat the oven to 350° F. Lightly grease 2 cookie sheets.

Shape the chilled dough into small balls and drop into a bowl containing the untoasted sesame seeds. Shake until the balls are well coated. Place on the cookie sheets, pressing flat with a fork. Bake for 12 minutes or until lightly browned. Let the cookies cool briefly before removing them to wire racks to cool completely.

Yield: 4 to 5 dozen cookies

Coffee Maple-Nut Crisscrosses

Hand-decorated with a fork, Crisscrosses have immediate eye-appeal, and a hint of coffee flavor makes them a natural after-dinner cookie.

2 cups unbleached all-purpose flour (or use half whole wheat pastry flour)
2 tablespoons instant coffee powder
1/2 teaspoon baking powder
1/8 teaspoon baking soda
1/4 teaspoon salt
2/3 cup (5 ounces) coarsely chopped dates, well packed
1/2 cup butter or margarine, melted
1/2 cup frozen apple juice concentrate, at room temperature
1 egg
1 teaspoon maple extract
1/2 cup chopped walnuts
1/4 cup finely chopped walnuts

In a large bowl, sift together the flour, coffee powder, baking powder, baking soda, and salt.

In a blender or food processor, puree the dates, melted butter, and apple juice concentrate. Blend in the egg and maple extract until just combined. Mix the date mixture with the dry ingredients. Add the 1/2 cup walnuts. If the dough is too sticky to handle, chill until firm.

Preheat the oven to 375° F. Lightly grease 2 cookie sheets.

Shape the dough into 1-inch balls. Place on the cookie sheets and flatten with a wet fork twice, pressing a crisscross pattern into each top. Sprinkle with 1/4 cup finely chopped walnuts. Bake for 15 minutes or until browned.

Let the cookies cool briefly before removing them to wire racks to cool completely.

Yield: 2-1/2 to 3 dozen cookies

Fruity Oatmeal Cookies

The apple juice and raisin sweeteners give a fruity overtone to these soft oatmeal cookies. Once you've tasted them you won't want to stop.

1/4 cup frozen apple juice concentrate

3/4 cup (6 ounces) coarsely chopped dates, well packed

1/2 cup butter or margarine

1 tablespoon grated orange rind

1/4 cup orange juice

1 teaspoon vanilla extract

3/4 cup unbleached all-purpose flour or whole wheat pastry flour

1/2 teaspoon baking soda

1-1/2 teaspoons cinnamon

1/4 teaspoon salt

1-1/2 cups rolled oats (noninstant)

1/2 cup raisins

1/2 cup walnuts

Preheat the oven to 325° F. Lightly grease 2 cookie sheets.

In a small saucepan, combine the apple juice concentrate and dates. Simmer until the dates are slightly softened, about 2 to 3 minutes. Add the butter, orange rind, orange juice, and vanilla, stirring until the butter is melted. Puree the mixture in a blender or food processor. Transfer to a bowl. Set aside to cool.

In a large bowl, sift together the flour, baking soda, cinnamon, and salt. Mix the date mixture with the dry ingredients. Blend in the rolled oats, raisins, and walnuts, mixing well.

Place heaping teaspoonfuls of the mixture 2 inches apart on the cookie sheets. Press with a wet spoon or spatula to flatten. Bake for 15 to 20 minutes or until browned.

Let the cookies cool briefly before removing them to wire racks to cool completely.

Yield: 2-1/2 to 3 dozen cookies

Cocoa-Orange Macaroons

A moist, chewy cookie that blends the zest of oranges with cocoa, dates, and coconut. These macaroons are a chewy solution to a chocolate craving. Share these easily transported cookies with friends and family in faraway places.

1 tablespoon unbleached all-purpose flour

3 tablespoons unsweetened powdered cocoa

1/4 cup nonfat dry milk powder

1/2 teaspoon cinnamon

2 egg whites, at room temperature

1/8 teaspoon cream of tartar

1/8 teaspoon salt

1/4 cup frozen apple juice concentrate, at room temperature

1 tablespoon grated orange rind

1/2 teaspoon vanilla extract

3/4 cup (6 ounces) chopped dates, well packed

1/2 cup chopped almonds, toasted

1/2 cup unsweetened shredded coconut

Preheat the oven to 300° F. Lightly grease 1 cookie sheet.

In a small bowl, sift together the flour, cocoa, milk powder, and cinnamon. Set aside.

Beat the egg whites until foamy. Add the cream of tartar and salt. Continue beating until stiff but not dry. Beat in the apple juice concentrate, orange rind, and vanilla. Fold in the dry ingredients.

Gently fold in the dates, almonds, and coconut. Drop by the teaspoon onto the cookie sheet. Bake for 15 minutes.

Let the macaroons cool briefly before removing them to wire racks to cool completely.

Yield: 2 dozen macaroons

Banana Almond Clusters

The sweetness of raisins and bananas combine with puffed rice and crunchy almonds to make a delicate but chewy cookie.

1/2 cup frozen apple juice concentrate
1 cup raisins
1 cup mashed ripe bananas
1 egg
1/3 cup vegetable oil
1 teaspoon grated orange rind
1/2 teaspoon almond extract
1 cup whole wheat pastry flour
1/2 teaspoon baking soda
1/4 teaspoon salt
1 teaspoon nutmeg
1-1/2 cups unsweetened puffed rice
2/3 cup chopped almonds

Preheat the oven to 300° F. Grease 2 cookie sheets.

In a small saucepan, heat the apple juice concentrate and raisins until the raisins are softened and puffed. Puree the mixture in a blender or food processor. Add the bananas, egg, oil, orange rind, and almond extract. Blend until just combined. Set aside to cool.

In a large bowl, sift together the flour, baking soda, salt, and nutmeg. Combine the banana mixture with the dry ingredients. Mix in the puffed rice and almonds. Drop from a teaspoon onto the cookie sheets. Bake for 15 to 18 minutes.

Let the cookies cool briefly before removing them to wire racks to cool completely. Store in the refrigerator or freezer.

Yield: 4 dozen cookies

Fruited Meringue Mounds

These soft meringue cookies are sweetened with confetti-like bits of dried fruit. They are most appealing right out of the oven.

1/3 cup finely chopped
   dried apricots
1/3 cup finely chopped raisins
1/3 cup finely chopped dates
2/3 cup rolled oats
   (noninstant)
2/3 cup unsweetened
   shredded coconut or
   shredded wheat cereal
2 tablespoons unbleached
   all-purpose flour
1 tablespoon grated orange
   rind
3 egg whites, at room
   temperature
1/4 teaspoon cream
   of tartar
1/8 teaspoon salt
4 tablespoons frozen apple
   juice concentrate, at room
   temperature
1/2 cup nonfat dry milk
   powder
1 teaspoon vanilla extract

Preheat the oven to 300° F. Grease and flour 2 cookie sheets.

Toss the dried fruits with the oats and coconut. Work in the flour and orange rind.

In another bowl, beat the egg whites until foamy. Add the cream of tartar and salt. Continue beating until stiff but not dry. Add the apple juice concentrate, powdered milk, and vanilla, beating until well combined. Fold the dried fruit into the beaten egg white mixture. Drop from a teaspoon onto the prepared cookie sheets. Bake for 20 minutes, or until golden brown.

Let the cookies cool briefly on cookie sheets. Serve them while still warm.

Yield: 3 dozen cookies

Pear Giants

Children love to help with these over-sized cookies, their eyes growing as big as saucers in anticipation. If your dried fruit is very stiff, briefly simmer or soak in apple juice to soften it. Drain before adding to the dough.

1 cup unbleached all-
 purpose flour
1 cup whole wheat pastry
 flour
1/2 teaspoon baking powder
1/2 teaspoon baking soda
1/4 teaspoon salt
1-1/4 teaspoons nutmeg
1 tablespoon grated orange
 rind
1-1/2 cups chopped dried
 pears
3/4 cup raisins
1/2 cup chopped pecans
1 cup (8 ounces) coarsely
 chopped dates, well packed
1/2 cup frozen apple juice
 concentrate, at room
 temperature
1/2 cup butter or margarine,
 at room temperature
1/4 cup unsweetened crunchy
 or smooth peanut butter
2 eggs
1 teaspoon vanilla extract
1 cup grated fresh pear
 (peeling optional)
Pecan halves

Preheat the oven to 350° F. Lightly grease 2 or 3 cookie sheets.

In a large bowl, sift together the flours, baking powder, baking soda, salt, and nutmeg. Stir in the orange rind, dried pears, raisins, and nuts, mixing until evenly distributed.

In a blender or food processor, puree the dates and apple juice concentrate. Blend in the butter, peanut butter, eggs, and vanilla until just combined. Mix the date mixture with the dry ingredients, along with the fresh pear.

For each cookie, place 1/4 cup dough onto a cookie sheet. Using the back of a spoon, spread the cookie until it measures 4 to 5 inches. Top each with pecan half. Bake for 25 minutes.

Let the cookies cool briefly before removing them to wire racks to cool completely.

Yield: 20 to 24 extra-large cookies

Baby Pear Giants. Drop dough by the tablespoon onto cookie sheets. Bake for 20 to 25 minutes. Makes 4 dozen.

Stuffed Date Drops

A walnut-stuffed date is baked inside a buttery cookie batter. These look mysterious until you take a bite. Glazed Oranges (page 182) make a nice counterpoint to the sweetness of these dates.

1 pound pitted whole dates
Approximately 48 large
   walnut pieces
1-1/4 cups whole wheat
   pastry flour
1/2 teaspoon baking powder
1/2 teaspoon baking soda
1/8 teaspoon salt
1/4 cup butter or margarine,
   at room temperature
1 egg, at room temperature
1/2 cup frozen apple juice
   concentrate, at room
   temperature
1 teaspoon grated orange
   rind
1/2 cup low-fat sour cream
   or nonfat yogurt

Stuff each date with a walnut piece. Preheat the oven to 350° F. Lightly grease 2 cookie sheets.

Sift together the flour, baking powder, baking soda, and salt.

In a large bowl, beat together the butter, egg, apple juice concentrate, and orange rind. The mixture will look lumpy. Mix in the dry ingredients, along with the sour cream, until just combined. Add a few stuffed dates at a time and stir until coated with the batter. Remove with a spoon and place, one by one, on the cookie sheets 2 inches apart. Bake for 15 minutes or until the tops of the cookies are golden and the edges slightly browned.

Let the Date Drops cool for 5 minutes before removing them to wire racks to cool completely.

Yield: 4 dozen cookies

Walnut Date Bars

Walnut Date Bars are easy to take along for morning meetings or a coffee klatch.

1/2 cup unbleached all-purpose flour
1/4 cup whole wheat pastry flour
1/2 teaspoon baking powder
1 teaspoon cinnamon
1/2 teaspoon allspice
1/2 teaspoon nutmeg
1/8 teaspoon salt
1/4 cup wheat germ
1 cup rolled oats (noninstant)
1-1/2 cups (12 ounces) coarsely chopped dates, well packed
1/2 cup melted butter or margarine
1/2 cup unsweetened apple butter (see page 187)
1 egg
2 tablespoons milk
1/4 cup frozen apple juice concentrate, at room temperature
1 teaspoon vanilla extract
1 cup chopped walnuts

Preheat the oven to 350° F. Grease a 13-inch by 9-inch baking pan.

In a large bowl, sift together the flours, baking powder, cinnamon, allspice, nutmeg, and salt. Stir in the wheat germ, oats, and 1 cup of the dates, mixing until evenly distributed.

In a blender or food processor, puree the remaining 1/2 cup dates and butter. Blend in the apple butter, egg, milk, apple juice concentrate, and vanilla until just combined. Stir the pureed date mixture into the dry ingredients.

Press the dough into the pan. Sprinkle evenly with the chopped walnuts, pressing lightly to cover the dough. Bake for 30 minutes.

Let the bars cool briefly before cutting them into rectangles with a sharp knife. Remove the bars to wire racks to cool completely. Store in the refrigerator or freezer.

Yield: 36 bars

Pecan Bark

These thin squares of pastry are loaded with pecans and dates.

2 tablespoons warm water
(105° F. to 115° F.)
1 envelope dry yeast
(1 tablespoon)
1-1/2 cups unbleached all-
purpose flour (or 1 cup
white and 1/2 cup whole
wheat)
1/4 teaspoon salt
2 teaspoons cinnamon
1/3 cup butter or margarine
1/4 cup nonfat dry milk
powder
1/2 cup apple juice
concentrate, at room
temperature
1 egg yolk
2/3 cup (5 ounces) finely
chopped dates, well packed
1-1/2 cups chopped pecans

Measure the warm water into a medium-sized bowl and sprinkle the yeast over it. Let stand for 5 minutes, then stir to dissolve.

In a large bowl, combine the flour, salt, and cinnamon. With a pastry blender or your fingers, cut in the butter or margarine until the mixture is coarse and crumbly.

In another bowl, combine the dry milk, apple juice concentrate, and egg yolk. Stir into the dissolved yeast. Add to the dry ingredients, beating until combined.

Toss the dates and nuts together until they are evenly distributed, then work them into dough. Cover the bowl tightly and refrigerate for 2 hours or overnight.

Preheat the oven to 325° F. Lightly grease 2 cookie sheets.

Divide the dough in half. Roll out half between 2 sheets of waxed paper until it measures 9 inches by 12 inches. The dough will be stiff. Remove the top sheet of waxed paper and flip the dough onto a cookie sheet. Peel off the remaining waxed paper. Repeat with the other half of dough.

Bake for 15 minutes, or until lightly browned. Remove the pan from the oven and cut while hot into 3-inch squares.

Let the cookies cool briefly before removing them to wire racks to cool completely.

Yield: 2 dozen cookies

Glazed Fruit Bars

An iced bar cookie packed with bits of raisins and nuts. Glazed Fruit Bars travel well, so if you'd like to give them as gifts, place the cookies on foil-covered cardboard and score them into diagonal bars, but don't cut all the way through.

FRUIT BARS

2 cups unbleached all-
  purpose flour (or use half
  whole wheat flour)
1-1/2 teaspoons cinnamon
2 teaspoons baking powder
1/2 teaspoon salt
1 cup (8 ounces) coarsely
  chopped dates, well packed
1 cup frozen apple juice
  concentrate, at room
  temperature
1/2 cup butter or margarine,
  melted
2 eggs
1 teaspoon vanilla extract
1 cup chopped raisins
1 cup chopped walnuts
2 teaspoons grated orange
  rind
2 tablespoons orange juice

GLAZE

1/2 cup nonfat dry milk
  powder
2 tablespoons frozen apple
  juice concentrate, at room
  temperature
1 teaspoon grated lemon
  rind
2 teaspoons lemon juice
1/4 teaspoon vanilla extract
2 teaspoons butter or
  margarine, melted

Preheat the oven to 375° F. Lightly grease 1 cookie sheet.

Sift together the flour, cinnamon, baking powder, and salt.

In a blender or food processor, puree 1/2 cup of the dates with apple juice concentrate and butter. Add the eggs and vanilla, blending until just combined. Transfer to a bowl and add the remaining 1/2 cup dates, along with the raisins, walnuts, and orange rind. Mix in the dry ingredients and orange juice, stirring until combined.

Divide the dough into 4 portions. Shape each portion into a narrow rectangle about 9 inches by 2 inches by 1/2 inch on the greased cookie sheet. Bake for 15 to 20 minutes.

Let the cookies cool completely on wire racks while you prepare the glaze. Combine all the glaze ingredients. When the cookies have cooled, spread the glaze over the tops of each rectangle. Cut them diagonally into 3/4-inch bars.

Yield: 2 dozen fruit bars

Ginger Snaps with a Bite

Ginger snaps are like Pepparkakors, *a Swedish cookie infused with ginger, cinnamon, and cloves. The spice flavors intensify if the ginger snaps are allowed to mellow for at least a day. Use this dough to make fancy cut-outs for eating, decorating a tree, or building a gingerbread house.*

1 cup unbleached all-
purpose flour
1 cup whole wheat pastry
flour
1 tablespoon ground ginger
1 teaspoon cinnamon
1/4 teaspoon ground cloves
1/4 teaspoon salt
1/2 cup dried currants
3/4 cup (6 ounces) coarsely
chopped dates, well packed
1/2 cup frozen apple juice
concentrate, at room
temperature
1/3 cup butter or margerine,
at room temperature
3 ounces low-fat cream
cheese, at room
temperature

In a large bowl, sift together the flours, ginger, cinnamon, cloves, and salt. Stir in the currants.

In a blender or food processor, puree the dates and apple juice concentrate. Blend in the butter and cream cheese until just combined. Stir the date mixture into the dry ingredients.

Flatten the dough into 2 thick pancakes. (If crumbly, sprinkle with a little water.) If necessary chill until firm enough to roll.

Preheat the oven to 325° F. Lightly grease 2 cookie sheets.

Roll out the dough 1/8 inch thick between 2 sheets of waxed paper. Cut into fancy shapes and place on greased cookie sheets. (Or shape the dough into 1-inch balls, place on the cookie sheets, and flatten with the heel of your hand.) Bake for 12 to 15 minutes, or until lightly browned.

Let the cookies cool briefly before removing them to wire racks to cool completely.

Yield: 2 to 4 dozen

Raisin' Hopes

The recipe for Raisin' Hopes was inspired by the old-fashioned sultana cookie. Be sure and take these along on your next picnic.

1/2 cup frozen apple juice concentrate
2/3 cup golden raisins
5 tablespoons butter or margarine, at room temperature
1 teaspoon vanilla extract
1 cup unbleached all-purpose flour
1 cup whole wheat pastry flour
1 teaspoon baking powder
1/4 teaspoon salt
1 teaspoon cinnamon
1 cup dark raisins
1 egg
1 teaspoon frozen apple juice concentrate, at room temperature

In a small saucepan, combine the apple juice concentrate and golden raisins. Simmer until the raisins are slightly softened, 2 to 3 minutes. Stir in the butter and vanilla. Puree the mixture in a blender or food processor until just combined. Transfer to a bowl. Set aside to cool.

In a large bowl, sift together the flours, baking powder, salt, and cinnamon. Stir in the dark raisins. Mix the pureed raisin mixture with the dry ingredients. If necessary, add a little water until the dough holds together.

Preheat the oven to 375° F. Lightly grease 2 cookie sheets, rimless if possible.

Turn the dough onto a lightly floured board and knead several times to incorporate as many of the dark raisins as possible. Divide the dough in half. Place each half directly on a cookie sheet and pat or roll out with a floured rolling pin to a thickness of 1/8 inch or until dough measures 9 inches by 12 inches. Using a sharp knife, trim ragged edges. Cut the dough into squares or any desired shapes. Brush with an egg wash made by beating the egg with the 1 teaspoon apple juice concentrate. Bake for 15 to 18 minutes or until lightly browned.

Let the cookies cool for 5 minutes before removing them to wire racks to cool completely.

Yield: 4 to 5 dozen

Apple-Fig Bars

These are our version of fig newtons. Keep them on hand for after school appetites or bedtime snacks. They pack well into picnic baskets.

FILLING

1-3/4 cups finely chopped
dried figs
1/3 cup frozen apple juice
concentrate
1 cup water
1 tablespoon lemon juice
2 teaspoons grated lemon
rind
2 teaspoons grated orange
rind

PASTRY

3/4 cup unbleached all-
purpose flour
1/2 cup whole wheat pastry
flour
1/4 teaspoon baking soda
1/8 teaspoon salt
1/4 cup butter or margarine,
at room temperature
1/4 cup unsweetened apple
butter (see page 202)
1 egg yolk
1 tablespoon frozen apple
juice concentrate, at room
temperature
1 teaspoon vanilla extract
1 tablespoon grated orange
rind

To make the filling, combine the figs, apple juice concentrate, and water in a saucepan. Simmer, uncovered, for 20 minutes or until the mixture has the consistency of jam. Stir in the lemon juice and lemon and orange rinds and set aside to cool while you prepare the pastry.

To make the pastry, sift together the flours, soda, and salt. In a large bowl, combine the butter, apple butter, and egg yolk and beat until creamy. Add the apple juice concentrate, vanilla, and orange rind; work together with a fork. Mix in the dry ingredients, stirring until well combined.

Preheat the oven to 375° F. Lightly grease 1 cookie sheet.

Turn the dough onto a floured surface and knead a few times to make a smooth ball. Place the dough between two sheets of waxed paper and roll it into a rectangle measuring 11 inches by 14 inches. Cut into 4 crosswise strips, each about 3-1/2 inches by 11 inches. Spoon a fourth of the filling down the center of each strip. Fold in the sides and press together to enclose filling. Place seam-side down on the cookie sheet and cut each strip into 6 pieces. Bake for 15 to 20 minutes.

Remove the bars to wire racks to cool completely. Store in the refrigerator or freezer.

Yield: 24 bars

Date-Apricot Bars

A tantalizing apricot-date filling lies between the layers of a crunchy oatmeal crust. Serve these as cookies or cut them into larger portions to make a special dessert.

FILLING

2 cups chopped dried apricots
2 cups (1 pound) chopped dates, well packed
2 teaspoons grated orange rind
1 cup apple juice (or 1/3 cup frozen apple juice concentrate and 2/3 cup water)
1/2 cup chopped walnuts

CRUST

2 cups rolled oats (noninstant)
1-1/2 cups whole wheat pastry flour
1/2 teaspoon baking soda
1/2 teaspoon allspice
1/8 teaspoon salt
1/2 cup butter or margarine, at room temperature
1/4 cup unsweetened apple butter (see page 202) or unsweetened applesauce (see page 187)
1/4 cup frozen apple juice concentrate, at room temperature

To make the filling, combine the apricots, dates, and orange rind with the apple juice in a saucepan. Bring to a boil, reduce the heat, and simmer, covered, for 5 minutes or until mixture is thick. Add the walnuts and set aside to cool.

Preheat the oven to 350° F. Lightly grease a 13-inch by 9-inch baking pan.

To make the crust, combine the rolled oats, flour, baking soda, allspice, and salt. Add the butter and mix until crumbly. Add the apple butter or applesauce and apple juice concentrate. Stir to combine. Divide into 2 equal parts.

Using the back of a spoon, press half of the crust mixture into the pan. Spread the filling over the crust. Dot the remaining crust on top, pressing lightly to cover the filling. Bake for 30 to 35 minutes.

Let the bars cool briefly before cutting them into rectangles with a sharp knife. Remove the bars to wire racks to cool completely. Store in the refrigerator or freezer.

Yield: 30 to 40 bars

Crusty Apple Butter Bars

Every bite of these bars tastes like apple pie. Serve with a hot, spicy tea.

CRUST

1 cup whole wheat pastry
  flour
1/2 cup unbleached all-
  purpose flour
1 cup crumbled shredded
  wheat cereal
1/2 teaspoon allspice
1/4 teaspoon salt
2/3 cup (5 ounces) coarsely
  chopped dates, well packed
1/2 cup melted butter or
  margarine

FILLING

2 cups unsweetened apple
  butter (see page 202)
1 cup raisins
1 cup chopped pecans

Preheat the oven to 350° F. Grease a 13-inch by 9-inch baking pan.

To make the crust, mix the flours, shredded wheat, allspice, and salt in a large bowl. Set aside. In a blender or food processor, puree the dates and butter. Mix the date mixture with the dry ingredients, stirring to blend. Divide into 2 equal parts. Press half of the dough evenly into the pan.

To make the filling, mix together the apple butter and raisins. Spoon the mixture evenly over first layer of dough. Mix the nuts into remaining half of dough and crumble it evenly over filling. Press the layers together lightly. Bake for 35 minutes or until golden brown.

Let the cookie cool briefly before cutting it into rectangles with a sharp knife. Remove the bars to wire racks to cool completely. Store in the refrigerator or freezer.

Yield: 36 bars

Anise Seed Cut-Outs

The anise flavor is especially delicious with a cup of tea, and it will intensify a day after baking.

1-1/2 cups unbleached all-purpose flour (or use half whole wheat pastry flour)

2 teaspoons cinnamon

1 to 1-1/2 tablespoons whole anise seed

1/4 teaspoon salt

1/2 cup (4 ounces) coarsely chopped dates, well packed

3 tablespoons frozen apple juice concentrate, at room temperature

1/2 cup butter or margarine, at room temperature

1 egg

1 teaspoon grated lemon rind

1 egg

1 teaspoon frozen apple juice concentrate, at room temperature

In a large bowl, stir together flour, cinnamon, anise, and salt.

In a blender or food processor, puree the dates and 3 tablespoons apple juice concentrate. Blend in the butter. Blend in the egg and lemon rind until just combined. Mix the date mixture with the dry ingredients, stirring to blend. Form into a ball, adding more flour if the mixture is too sticky. If necessary, chill the dough until it is firm enough to roll.

Preheat the oven to 375° F. Lightly grease 2 cookie sheets.

Roll out the dough to a thickness of 1/8 inch on a lightly floured board. Cut into fancy shapes. Place on the cookie sheets and brush with an egg wash made by beating the egg with the remaining 1 teaspoon apple juice concentrate. Bake for 10 to 15 minutes.

Let the cookies cool briefly before removing them to wire racks to cool completely.

Yield: 3 dozen

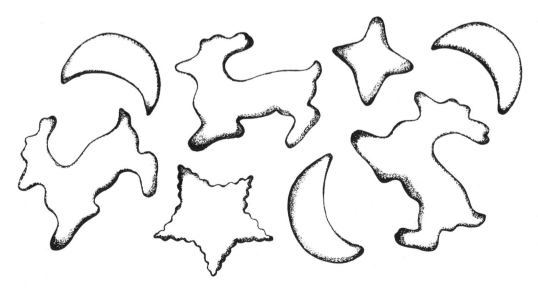

Spicy Icebox Cookies

This dough can be made ahead and refrigerated or frozen until you are ready to bake. The flavor of the spices will increase over time.

1-1/4 cups whole wheat
  pastry flour
3/4 cup finely chopped
  almonds
1 teaspoon cinnamon
1 teaspoon ground cloves
1 teaspoon nutmeg
1 teaspoon allspice
1 tablespoon unsweetened
  powdered cocoa
1/8 teaspoon salt
1 cup (8 ounces) finely
  chopped dates, well packed
1/4 cup finely chopped raisins
1 teaspoon grated orange rind
1/2 cup butter or margarine,
  softened
1/2 cup frozen apple juice
  concentrate, at room
  temperature
1 egg yolk
1 teaspoon vanilla extract

In a large bowl, stir together the flour, almonds, spices, cocoa, and salt. Add the dates, raisins, and orange rind, mixing to evenly distribute. Add the butter, blending it in with a fork. Stir in the apple juice concentrate, egg yolk, and vanilla, blending well.

Form into rolls 1-1/2 inches by 9 inches long, wrap, and chill in the freezer for 45 minutes, or until very firm.

Preheat the oven to 375° F. Grease 2 cookie sheets.

When the dough is thoroughly chilled, cut into 1/8-inch slices. Use a very sharp knife and a gentle sawing motion. Wipe the knife frequently to keep the slices uniform. Place the cookies on the cookie sheets and bake for 10 to 12 minutes, or until lightly browned.

Let the cookies cool briefly before removing them to wire racks to cool completely.

Yield: 4 dozen

Cheesecake Cookies

Just the right cookie for cheesecake lovers, these can be bite-sized or cut into larger portions. Serve with fresh strawberries.

CRUST

1/3 cup (2-1/2 ounces) coarsely chopped dates, well packed
1/3 cup melted butter or margarine
1 cup unbleached all-purpose flour
1/2 cup finely chopped walnuts

TOPPING

1/3 cup (2-1/2 ounces) coarsely chopped dates, well packed
3 tablespoons frozen apple juice concentrate, at room temperature
1 egg
1 teaspoon vanilla extract
2 teaspoons grated lemon rind
8 ounces low-fat cream cheese, at room temperature

Preheat the oven to 325° F. Grease an 8-inch by 8-inch baking pan.

To make the crust, puree the dates and butter in a blender or food processor. Transfer the mixture to a bowl and stir in the flour and nuts until texture resembles coarse meal. Set aside 3/4 cup. Press the remaining mixture into the prepared pan. Bake for 12 minutes and remove from the oven. Let cool for 5 minutes.

To make the topping, puree the dates and apple juice concentrate in a food processor or blender. Blend in the egg, vanilla, lemon rind, and cream cheese until just combined. Spread the mixture over the baked crust. Sprinkle the reserved crumbs over the top, pressing lightly. Bake for 25 minutes.

Let the cookies cool briefly before cutting them into squares with a sharp knife. Remove the cookies to wire racks to cool completely. Store in the refrigerator or freezer.

Yield: 25 squares

Crunch-Top Apple Sesame Squares

These are tempting morsels filled with apple flavor and sesame crunch. Try serving them with Pineapple Pudding (page 166).

FILLING

2 cups finely chopped, unpeeled raw apple

1/2 cup chopped dried apple

1/2 cup raisins

1 cup apple juice (or 1/3 cup frozen apple juice concentrate and 2/3 cup water)

2 teaspoons cinnamon

2 teaspoons grated lemon rind

PASTRY

1 cup unbleached all-purpose flour

1/2 cup whole wheat pastry flour

1/2 cup ground walnuts or almonds

1 teaspoon cinnamon

1/4 teaspoon salt

1/2 cup (4 ounces) coarsely chopped dates, well packed

6 tablespoons melted butter or margarine

2 tablespoons frozen apple juice concentrate

1 teaspoon vanilla extract

1/3 cup sesame seeds

To make the filling, combine the raw and dried apple, raisins, apple juice, cinnamon, and lemon rind in a small saucepan. Bring to a boil, reduce the heat, and simmer for 5 to 10 minutes or until the mixture is thick and the liquid is absorbed. Set aside to cool.

Preheat the oven to 350° F. Lightly grease a 9-inch by 9-inch baking pan.

To make the pastry, stir together the flours, ground nuts, cinnamon, and salt in a bowl; set aside. In a blender or food processor, puree the dates and butter. Blend in the apple juice concentrate and vanilla until combined. Mix the date mixture with the dry ingredients, stirring to blend.

Press the pastry into the baking pan, spreading it 1/2 inch up the sides. Smooth the filling evenly over the crust. Sprinkle with the sesame seeds. Bake for 20 to 25 minutes.

Let the cookies cool briefly before cutting them into squares with a sharp knife. Remove the cookies to wire racks to cool completely. Store in the refrigerator or freezer.

Yield: 25 squares

Turkish Wheat Crispies

A rich date and nut mixture is layered between crumbled, shredded wheat and drizzled with a syrupy orange glaze. Enjoy these the traditional Turkish way with a cup of mint tea.

ORANGE SYRUP

2 teaspoons grated orange
  rind
1-1/2 cups orange juice
1/2 cup frozen apple juice
  concentrate

3 cups crumbled shredded
  wheat cereal

NUT FILLING

1 cup ground walnuts
1 cup ground almonds
1/2 cup (4 ounces) finely
  chopped dates, well packed
1 tablespoon cinnamon
1/8 teaspoon salt
1 teaspoon grated lemon
  rind
1/4 cup frozen apple juice
  concentrate

2 tablespoons butter or
  margarine, melted

Thoroughly grease a 9-inch by 9-inch baking pan.

To make the orange syrup, combine the orange rind, orange juice, and apple juice concentrate in a small saucepan. Bring to a boil, reduce the heat, and simmer over very low heat for 10 minutes. Set aside.

Preheat the oven to 350° F.

Sprinkle half of the shredded wheat evenly into pan. Spoon half of the hot orange syrup over it.

To make the nut filling, work with your fingers or a fork to combine the nuts, dates, cinnamon, salt, lemon rind, and apple juice concentrate. Crumble the mixture evenly over the shredded wheat. Top with the remaining shredded wheat. Press the layers together lightly. Spoon over the remaining orange syrup. Drizzle with melted butter. Bake for 30 to 35 minutes, or until golden brown.

Let the cookies cool briefly before cutting them into 1-1/2-inch squares with a very sharp knife. Remove the cookies to wire racks to cool completely. Serve in paper pastry cups. Store in in the refrigerator or freezer.

Yield: 36 squares

Turkish Nut Balls. Mix together the nut filling mixture as above. Shape into small balls. Beat 1 egg white with a fork, just until foamy. Dip each ball into egg white, then roll in crumbled shredded wheat. Place on a greased cookie sheet and bake in a 350° F. oven for 12 minutes. Makes 24 to 30 balls.

Mosaics

These candy-like confections are crunchy with nuts and flavored with orange rind. Add these to your dessert tray the next time you have a party or put them in decorative wrappers and give them as gifts.

1/2 cup raisins
1/3 cup pitted prunes
1 cup (8 ounces) dates, well packed
1/4 cup dried apricots
1 tablespoon grated orange rind
1 teaspoon grated lemon rind
1/4 cup finely chopped walnuts

Combine the fruits. Process in a food processor or put through a food grinder until minced. Add the orange and lemon rind and mix until well combined. Form into a roll about 1-1/2 inches by 7 inches. Roll in the chopped walnuts. Chill thoroughly and cut into slices. Store in an airtight container in the refrigerator.

Yield: 28 to 30 slices

Nutty Peanut Butter Nuggets

Finely ground fruits form the chewy centers of these sesame-coated morsels. No baking required.

3/4 cup chopped dried figs
1/4 cup raisins
1/2 cup walnuts, finely
  chopped
1 teaspoon grated orange
  rind
1/2 cup unsalted,
  unsweetened crunchy
  peanut butter
Toasted sesame seeds

Combine the figs and raisins. Process in a food processor or put through a food grinder until minced. Place in a bowl and add the walnuts, orange rind, and peanut butter, mixing until well combined. Form into small balls. Roll in sesame seeds. Store in an airtight container in the refrigerator.

Yield: 24 to 30 nuggets

Dessert Breads, Muffins, & Coffeecakes

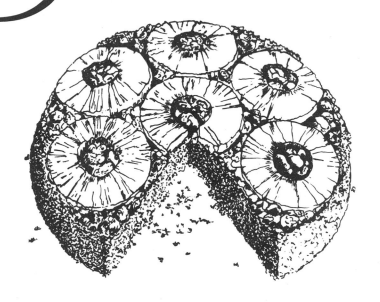

Quick breads and muffins truly are quick and easy to make. And, like coffeecakes, they lend themselves beautifully to the flavors of dried fruits, nuts, and whole wheat flours.

The trick with quick breads is to make them quickly. Dry ingredients should be well mixed and fluffed with a fork before you combine them with the liquid. This step lightens and aerates them, making them easier to combine. Don't overstir or your bread will be dense and heavy. Stir lightly, just enough to mix, even to the point of leaving a few small lumps. Work quickly to transfer the batter into a preheated oven.

Test for doneness about 5 minutes before the recipe says time is up. If the loaf springs back under gentle pressure from your fingertip and shows signs of pulling away from the sides of the pan, it may be done. You can double-check by inserting a toothpick deep into the center of the loaf. If it comes out clean, baking is completed.

To cool quick breads and muffins, remove them from the oven and place on wire racks where air can circulate

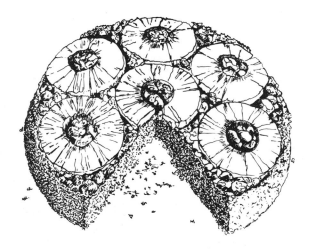

Dessert Breads, Muffins, and Coffeecakes   133

around them. Allow a baked loaf to cool in the pan for about 10 minutes, then remove it from the pan and place it on a rack to cool completely. If you wait several hours after cooling a quick bread, it will be less likely to crumble when sliced.

Most quick breads increase in flavor when wrapped and refrigerated overnight.

Store quick breads, muffins, and coffeecakes tightly wrapped in the refrigerator or freezer.

Tangerine Bread

This fragrant loaf is textured with flecks of tangerine peel, currants, and nuts. Oranges can be substituted when tangerines are not in season. As with most quick breads, the flavor will be enhanced if the loaf is refrigerated overnight before serving. Tangerine Bread is delicious toasted.

2 cups unbleached all-
purpose flour (or 1-1/2 cups
all-purpose and 1/2 cup
whole wheat)
2 teaspoons baking powder
1 teaspoon baking soda
1/2 teaspoon salt
1/2 cup dried currants
1/4 cup chopped nuts
3/4 cup seeded coarsely
chopped tangerine,
including peel
1/3 cup (2-1/2 ounces)
coarsely chopped dates,
well packed
1/4 cup frozen apple juice
concentrate, at room
temperature
2 tablespoons tangerine or
orange juice
1 egg, beaten
2/3 cup low-fat milk
1 tablespoon vegetable oil
1 teaspoon vanilla extract

Preheat the oven to 300° F. Lightly grease and flour a 9-inch by 5-inch loaf pan.

In a large bowl, sift together the flour, baking powder, baking soda, and salt. Stir in the currants and nuts.

In a blender or food processor, combine the tangerines, dates, apple juice concentrate, and tangerine juice. Process until the mixture is finely chopped. Set aside.

In another bowl, stir together the beaten egg, milk, oil, and vanilla. Add the tangerine mixture. Mix into the dry ingredients, stirring until just blended. Spoon into the prepared pan and bake for 45 to 50 minutes.

Cool on a wire rack for 10 minutes, then remove from the pan.

Yield: 1 loaf

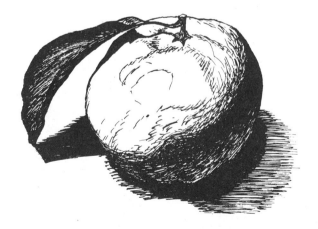

Banana Apricot Bread

Snips of apricot and orange contribute a large measure of flavor to this loaf. Use very ripe bananas to ensure the sweetness of this bread.

1 cup unbleached all-purpose flour
3/4 cup whole wheat flour
1-1/2 teaspoons baking powder
1/2 teaspoon baking soda
1/2 teaspoon salt
1 teaspoon cinnamon
2/3 cup (5 ounces) chopped dried apricots
1/2 cup chopped walnuts
1 tablespoon grated orange rind
1 cup mashed ripe banana
1/4 cup (2 ounces) coarsely chopped dates, well packed
1/2 cup frozen apple juice concentrate, at room temperature
1/3 cup vegetable oil
2 eggs
1/4 cup nonfat plain yogurt

Preheat the oven to 325° F. Lightly grease and flour an 8-inch by 4-inch loaf pan or three 5-1/2-inch by 3-1/2-inch miniature loaf pans.

In a large bowl, sift together the flours, baking powder, baking soda, salt, and cinnamon. Stir in the apricots, nuts, and orange rind.

In a blender or food processor, puree the banana, dates, and apple juice concentrate. Blend in the oil, eggs, and yogurt until just combined. Mix the banana mixture with the dry ingredients, stirring only enough to blend. Spoon into the prepared pan(s) and bake for 50 to 60 minutes in the single loaf pan or 35 to 40 minutes in the small loaf pans.

Cool on a wire rack for 10 minutes, then remove from the pan(s).

Yield: 1 loaf or 3 small loaves

Carrot-Fig Bread

It's amazing what moisture and sweetness carrots give to this loaf. Crunchy fig seeds and walnuts add an unusual texture.

1-3/4 cups unbleached all-purpose flour (or 1 cup all-purpose and 3/4 cup whole wheat)
1 teaspoon baking soda
1/4 teaspoon salt
1 teaspoon cinnamon
1 teaspoon nutmeg
1-1/2 cups finely grated carrots, lightly packed
3/4 cup chopped walnuts
1 cup chopped dried figs (use scissors to cut figs)
1/2 cup orange juice
2 eggs
2/3 cup frozen apple juice concentrate, at room temperature
1/3 cup vegetable oil
1 teaspoon vanilla extract

Preheat the oven to 325° F. Lightly grease and flour a 9-inch by 5-inch loaf pan or three 5-1/2-inch by 3-1/2-inch miniature loaf pans.

In a large bowl, sift together the flour, baking soda, salt, cinnamon, and nutmeg. Stir in the carrots and nuts.

In a small saucepan, simmer the figs in the orange juice until the liquid is absorbed and the figs are softened. Set aside to cool.

Beat the eggs until foamy. Stir in the apple juice concentrate, oil, and vanilla and continue to beat until well mixed. Stir in the softened figs. Mix the fig mixture with the dry ingredients, stirring just enough to blend. Spoon into the prepared pan(s). Bake for 55 to 65 minutes in the large loaf pan or 45 to 50 minutes in the miniature pans.

Cool on a wire rack for 10 minutes, then remove from the pan(s).

Yield: 1 large loaf or 3 miniature loaves

Spiced Tea Morning Loaf

A dark, sweet loaf to enjoy with a cup of tea. It gains in flavor if made a day in advance.

2 cups unbleached all-purpose flour (or 1-1/2 cups all-purpose and 1/2 cup whole wheat)
2 teaspoons baking powder
2 teaspoons baking soda
1/4 teaspoon salt
2 cups rolled oats (noninstant)
1 cup raisins
1 cup strong, hot, brewed spice tea
1 cup (8 ounces) coarsely chopped dates, well packed
1/4 cup butter or margarine
1-1/2 tablespoons grated orange rind
3/4 cup orange juice
1/2 cup frozen apple juice concentrate
2 eggs

Preheat the oven to 325° F. Lightly grease and flour a 9-inch by 5-inch loaf pan or three 5-1/2-inch by 3-1/2-inch loaf pans.

In a large bowl, sift together flour, baking powder, baking soda, and salt. Stir in rolled oats and raisins.

In a blender or food processor, combine the tea, dates, and butter. Blend until the dates are finely chopped. Blend in the orange rind, orange juice, apple juice concentrate, and eggs, until just combined.

Mix the date mixture with the dry ingredients, stirring just enough to blend. Spoon into the prepared pan(s). Bake for 1 hour in a single loaf pan and for 45 to 50 minutes in the miniature pans.

Cool on a wire rack for 10 minutes, then remove from the pan(s).

Yield: 1 large loaf or 3 small loaves

Pumpkin-Pecan Bread

Pumpkin and pecan, the flavors of autumn, mingle in this delicious bread. It is especially flavorful when served warm. Serve with Baked Fresh Fruit Compote (page 180).

2 cups unbleached all-purpose flour (or use 1 cup all-purpose and 1 cup whole wheat flour)
2 teaspoons baking soda
1/2 teaspoon salt
2 teaspoons cinnamon
1 teaspoon nutmeg
1/2 teaspoon ground cloves
1 cup rolled oats (noninstant)
1 cup chopped pecans
1/2 cup (4 ounces) coarsely chopped dates, well packed
3/4 cup frozen apple juice concentrate, at room temperature
1/3 cup vegetable oil
2 eggs
1 teaspoon vanilla extract
1 tablespoon grated orange rind
2 cups canned or cooked and strained pumpkin

Preheat the oven to 325° F. Lightly grease and flour a 9-inch tube pan or bundt pan or three 5 1/2 inch by 3-1/2-inch loaf pans.

In a large bowl, sift together the flour, baking soda, salt, cinnamon, nutmeg, and cloves. Stir in the oats and pecans.

In a blender or food processor, puree the dates, apple juice concentrate, and oil. Blend in the eggs, vanilla, and orange rind until just combined. Mix the date mixture with the dry ingredients, along with the pumpkin, stirring just enough to blend. Spoon into the prepared pan(s). Bake for 1-1/4 hours in the tube pan and 50 to 55 minutes in the miniature loaf pans.

Cool on a wire rack for 10 minutes, then remove from the pan(s).

Yield: 1 large ring or 3 small loaves

Persimmon Bread

We use the persimmon variety Hachiya, which is commonly found in produce departments in the late fall. It is usually large — 3 inches broad and 4 inches long — and it must be perfectly ripe or its flavor is very astringent. Wait until its red-orange skin becomes translucent and its flesh feels nearly liquid. The flesh freezes very well. Why not stock up during the height of the season and have the taste of this unusual bread when there is not a persimmon in sight? Bake in miniature loaf pans for gift-giving.

1 cup unbleached all-
   purpose flour (or use half
   whole wheat flour)
1-1/2 teaspoons baking
   powder
2 teaspoons baking soda
1 teaspoon cinnamon
1/2 teaspoon allspice
1 cup persimmon pulp
1 cup unsweetened apple
   butter (see page 202)
1 cup dark raisins
1 cup chopped nuts or
   sunflower seeds
1/4 cup milk
2 tablespoons butter or
   margarine, melted
1 teaspoon vanilla extract

Preheat the oven to 350° F. Lightly grease and flour an 8-inch by 8-inch baking pan or three 5-1/2-inch by 3-1/2-inch miniature loaf pans.

In a large bowl, sift together the flour, baking powder, baking soda, cinnamon, and allspice.

In another bowl, stir together the persimmon pulp and apple butter. Add the raisins, nuts, milk, melted butter, and vanilla. Mix the persimmon mixture with the dry ingredients, stirring until just blended. Spoon into the prepared pan(s). Bake for 1-1/4 to 1-1/2 hours in the 8-inch baking pan or for 1 to 1-1/4 hours in the miniature loaf pans.

Cool on a wire rack for 10 minutes, then remove from the pan(s).

Yield: 6 servings

Blueberry Muffins

These delicately sweet muffins are a good choice to accompany a fruit salad. For variety, we replace the blueberries with 3/4 cup dried currants. Serve with Whipped Cheese Topping (page 211) or Trim Topping (page 211).

1 3/4 cups unbleached all-purpose flour

1 teaspoon baking powder

1/2 teaspoon baking soda

1/4 teaspoon salt

1/2 teaspoon nutmeg

1/2 teaspoon cinnamon

3/4 cup coarsely chopped golden raisins

2/3 cup frozen apple juice concentrate

1/4 cup water

3 tablespoons butter or margarine

2 eggs

1/2 cup plain nonfat yogurt or low-fat sour cream

1-1/4 cups unsweetened blueberries, drained and lightly floured (fresh or frozen and defrosted)

Preheat the oven to 375° F. Lightly grease and flour 16 to 18 muffin cups.

In a large bowl, sift together the flour, baking powder, baking soda, salt, nutmeg, and cinnamon.

In a small saucepan, combine the raisins with the apple juice concentrate and water. Bring to a boil, then reduce the heat and simmer for 5 minutes. Puree the mixture in a blender or food processor. Blend in the butter. Blend in the eggs and yogurt until just combined. Mix the raisin mixture with the dry ingredients, stirring just enough to blend. Fold in the blueberries.

Fill the muffin cups two-thirds full. Bake for 20 to 25 minutes or until a toothpick inserted in the center of a muffin comes out clean.

Cool on a wire rack for 5 minutes, then remove the muffins from the pan.

Yield: 16 to 18 muffins

Hearty Oat Bran Muffins

For all their high-fiber ingredients, Oat Bran Muffins have a pleasant light texture and more than a hint of sweetness.

1-3/4 cups oat bran
1 cup whole wheat flour
2 teaspoons baking powder
1/2 teaspoon cinnamon
1/2 teaspoon salt
1 cup grated carrots, lightly packed
2/3 cup chopped mixed dried fruits (raisins, apricots, dates, prunes)
1/3 cup chopped walnuts or almonds
2 egg whites
1 cup low-fat milk
1/2 cup frozen apple juice concentrate, at room temperature
2 tablespoons vegetable oil

Preheat the oven to 375° F. Lightly grease 12 muffin cups.

In a large bowl, stir together the oat bran, flour, baking powder, cinnamon, and salt. Add the carrots, dried fruits, and nuts. Mix until evenly distributed. Make a well in the center.

In another bowl, beat the egg whites lightly. Mix in the milk, apple juice concentrate, and oil. Pour all at once into the dry ingredients and stir until just moistened. Spoon into greased muffin cups, filling them three-quarters full. Bake for 25 minutes.

Cool on a wire rack for 5 minutes, then remove from the pan.

Yield: 12 muffins

Pumpkin-Date Muffins

This is a golden, pebbly-topped muffin. Serve with Whipped Cheese Topping (page 211) or Trim Topping (page 211).

1 cup unbleached all-
    purpose flour
1/2 teaspoon baking powder
1/2 teaspoon baking soda
1/2 teaspoon cinnamon
1/2 teaspoon nutmeg
1/2 teaspoon ginger
1/4 teaspoon salt
1/2 cup (4 ounces) finely
    chopped dates, well packed
1/2 cup chopped walnuts
1/2 cup frozen apple juice
    concentrate
1/2 cup (4 ounces) coarsely
    chopped dates, well packed
1/4 cup butter or margarine
2 eggs
2/3 cup canned or cooked
    and strained pumpkin
1 teaspoon vanilla extract

Preheat the oven to 350° F. Lightly grease 24 muffin cups.

In a large bowl, sift together the flour, baking powder, baking soda, cinnamon, nutmeg, ginger, and salt. Stir in the finely chopped dates and walnuts.

In a small saucepan, combine the apple juice concentrate and coarsely chopped dates. Simmer until the dates are softened, about 2 minutes. Stir in the butter until it melts. Puree the mixture in a blender or food processor. Blend in the eggs, pumpkin, and vanilla until just combined. Add the pumpkin mixture to the dry ingredients, stirring just enough to blend. Spoon into the prepared muffin cups, filling about two-thirds full. Bake for 20 to 25 minutes.

Cool on a wire rack for 5 minutes, then remove the muffins from the pan.

Yield: 12 muffins

Apple Crumble Currant Coffeecake

The yeast in the recipe is quickly activated, and no kneading is required. The batter is mixed, allowed to rise once, and then baked. Allow an hour for the dough to rise.

COFFEECAKE

1-3/4 to 2-1/4 cups
unbleached all-purpose
flour (or use half whole
wheat flour)
1 package dry yeast
(1 tablespoon)
1/4 cup milk
1/4 cup butter or margarine
1/4 teaspoon salt
1/3 cup frozen apple juice
concentrate, warmed
2 eggs, at room temperature
1 cup currants
2 apples, peeled (optional),
cored, and thinly sliced

TOPPING

3/4 cup (6 ounces) chopped
dates, well packed
2 tablespoons frozen apple
juice concentrate, at room
temperature
3/4 cup finely ground dry
bread crumbs
2 teaspoons cinnamon
3 tablespoons butter or
margarine

Lightly grease a 9-inch by 9-inch baking pan.

In a mixing bowl, thoroughly combine 1 cup of the flour and the yeast.

Combine the milk, butter, and salt in a saucepan. Heat slowly until very warm (120° to 130° F.). Gradually add to the dry ingredients along with the apple juice concentrate. Beat for 2 minutes with an electric mixer at medium speed (or 300 strokes by hand.) Add the eggs and 1/2 to 1 cup of the remaining flour or enough to make a thick batter. Beat at high speed for 2 minutes (or 300 strokes by hand.) Stir in the currants and enough additional flour to make a stiff batter. Spread evenly into the pan. Arrange the apples over the batter.

To make the topping, blend the dates, apple juice concentrate, bread crumbs, cinnamon, and butter in a food processor or blender. Mix until crumbly. Sprinkle over the apples. Cover with a towel and let rise in a warm place until doubled in bulk, about 1 hour.

Preheat the oven to 350° F.

When the rising is completed, bake for 35 to 40 minutes.

Serve while still warm or transfer to a wire rack to cool.

Yield: 8 servings

Pineapple Upside-Down Coffeecake

Traditionally, an upside-down cake is baked in an iron skillet, but a layer cake pan will work, too. Whatever pan you choose, the aroma of pineapple escaping from the oven is the signal of good tastes to come. Serve Pineapple Upside-Down Cake as a coffeecake or as a dessert.

TOPPING

1 (20-ounce) can
  unsweetened sliced
  pineapple
3/4 cup golden raisins
1/4 cup frozen apple juice
  concentrate

CAKE

2 cups unbleached all-
  purpose flour (or 1 cup
  unbleached all-purpose
  and 1 cup whole wheat
  pastry flour)
1 teaspoon baking powder
1 teaspoon baking soda
1/4 teaspoon salt
2 teaspoons cinnamon
1/2 teaspoon ginger
1/2 cup (4 ounces) chopped
  dates, well packed
1/2 cup frozen apple juice
  concentrate, at room
  temperature
1/4 cup vegetable oil
2 eggs
1 cup nonfat yogurt or
  buttermilk
1 teaspoon vanilla extract

Preheat the oven to 350° F. Lightly grease a 9-inch iron skillet or heavy heatproof skillet; or use a cake pan with 2-inch sides.

To make the topping, drain the pineapple, reserving 2 tablespoons of the juice. Arrange 7 to 8 pineapple slices in the bottom of the skillet or cake pan. Cut the remaining pineapple slices into small chunks. Set aside on a paper towel to drain.

In a small saucepan, simmer the raisins, apple juice concentrate, and the 2 tablespoons pineapple juice, uncovered, for 5 minutes or until syrupy. Spoon the mixture over the pineapple slices, spreading the raisins into the empty spaces.

To make the cake, sift together the flour, baking powder, baking soda, salt, cinnamon, and ginger into a large bowl.

In a blender or food processor, puree the dates, apple juice concentrate, and oil. Blend in the eggs, yogurt, and vanilla until just combined. Mix the date mixture with the dry ingredients, along with the reserved pineapple chunks, stirring just enough to blend. Spoon the batter over the topping. Bake for 45 to 50 minutes.

Cool on a rack for 5 minutes, then run a knife around the edge, place a platter on top of the pan, and invert cake onto the platter. Serve while still warm.

Yield: 8 servings

Fruit-Filled Coffeecake Ring

This sweet yeast dough makes a pair of richly flavored coffeecake rings that can be filled with prune-apple or cinnamon-nut filling. The recipe also gives instructions for shaping the filled dough into rolls.

DOUGH

1/4 cup warm water (105° F.
    to 115° F.)
2 packages dry yeast
    (2 tablespoons)
1/2 cup low-fat milk
1/4 cup butter or margarine
1/2 cup frozen apple juice
    concentrate, at room
    temperature
1/2 teaspoon salt
1/2 teaspoon ground
    cardamom or allspice
2 eggs, lightly beaten
Approximately 4 cups
    unbleached all-purpose
    flour (or 3 cups unbleached
    all-purpose flour and 1 cup
    whole wheat flour)

PRUNE FILLING

2-1/2 cups chopped pitted
    prunes
3 cups finely chopped or
    grated apple
1 tablespoon grated lemon
    rind
1 teaspoon cinnamon
1 cup apple juice (or 1/3 cup
    frozen apple juice
    concentrate and 2/3 cup
    water)
1/2 cup chopped nuts

To make the dough, place the warm water in a large bowl and sprinkle the yeast over it. Let stand for 5 minutes, then stir to dissolve.

In a small saucepan, scald the milk; then remove from the heat, add the butter, and stir until dissolved. Add the apple juice concentrate, salt, and cardamom. Stir into the yeast mixture. Add the beaten eggs and 2 cups of the flour. Beat for 2 minutes with an electric mixer at medium speed (or 300 strokes by hand). Beat until smooth. Stir in enough additional flour to make a slightly stiff dough. Turn out onto a lightly floured board. Knead until smooth and elastic, about 8 minutes. Place in a greased bowl, turning to grease top. Cover and let rise in a warm place until doubled, about 1 hour. Meanwhile, prepare filling.

To prepare the prune filling, combine the prunes, apples, lemon rind, cinnamon, and apple juice in a small saucepan and cook over low heat until the prunes are softened and mixture is thickened, about 15 minutes. Stir occasionally. Cool and add the nuts. Set aside.

Lightly grease 2 cookie sheets.

To make the rings, punch the dough down and divide it in half. On a lightly floured board, roll one half at a time into a 10-inch by 16-inch rectangle. Spread it with half of the filling mixture. Roll it up starting at the bottom of the long side to form a 16-inch roll. Pinch along the seam to seal. Lift the roll onto a cookie sheet with the seam-side down and form it into a ring. Pinch the ends together. With scissors make cuts 2/3 through the top surface at 1-inch intervals. Repeat this process with the remaining dough and filling. Cover the rings and let them rise until doubled, about 1 hour.

Preheat the oven to 325° F. Prepare the egg wash by beating the egg yolk with the apple juice concentrate.

EGG WASH

1 egg yolk
1 teaspoon frozen apple juice concentrate, at room temperature

Brush the egg wash over the rings. Bake for 25 minutes or until golden. Remove the rings from the baking sheets and allow them to cool on wire racks.

To make rolls, preheat the oven to 325° F. and prepare the egg wash as above. After forming the two 16-inch rolls, cut into 1-inch slices and place them in greased muffin pans or 1 inch apart on greased baking sheets. (Those baked in muffin pans will be high and those baked on baking sheets will be flatter.) Cover the rolls and let them rise until they are doubled in size, about 45 minutes. Brush with the egg wash. Bake for 20 to 25 minutes. Serve the rolls warm or transfer them to wire racks to cool.

Yield: 2 rings or 32 rolls

Cinnamon-Nut Coffeecake Ring. Prepare the coffeecake as above, substituting a cinnamon-nut filling for the prune filling. To make the cinnamon-nut filling, combine 2 cups raisins, 1 cup finely ground dry bread crumbs, 1 cup chopped walnuts, 2 teaspoons cinnamon, 1/2 teaspoon nutmeg, 2 tablespoons melted butter, 2 tablespoons milk, and 2 tablespoons frozen apple juice concentrate, at room temperature.

Alsatian Fruit Bread

This aromatic holiday bread originated in Alsace, a region in northeastern France. Each slice reveals a mosaic of colorful dried fruits.

The fruits must be prepared 1 day ahead to allow them to soften in the fruit juice. On the second day, 2-1/2-hours preparation time is needed for the dough to rise.

DAY 1

1-1/2 cups diced dried pears
1 cup raisins
1/2 cup diced dried figs
1/3 cup diced prunes
1-1/4 cups frozen apple
   juice concentrate
1/4 cup water
1 teaspoon grated lemon
   rind

DAY 2

3/4 cup warm water (105° F.
   to 115° F.)
1 package dry yeast
   (1 tablespoon)
1/2 cup lukewarm low-fat
   or whole milk
1 egg, lightly beaten
2 teaspoons cinnamon
1 teaspoon whole anise seeds
1/2 teaspoon salt
3-1/2 to 4-1/2 cups
   unbleached all-purpose
   flour (or use half whole
   wheat flour)
3/4 cup toasted chopped
   almonds
3/4 cup toasted walnuts

Combine the pears, raisins, figs, and prunes in a bowl. Heat the apple juice concentrate, water, and lemon rind until very hot. Stir into the fruit and let stand overnight, stirring occasionally.

The next day, place the 3/4 cup water in a small bowl and sprinkle the yeast over it. Let stand for 5 minutes, then stir to dissolve.

In a large bowl, combine the dissolved yeast with the milk, egg, cinnamon, anise, and salt. Mix well. Gradually stir in enough of the flour (2-1/2 to 3 cups) to make a soft dough. Knead the dough on a well-floured surface, adding only as much of the remaining flour as needed, reserving the rest for later. When the dough is stiff and elastic, shape into a smooth ball. Place in a greased bowl, turning over once to grease top. Cover with a towel and let rise until doubled, about 1 hour.

Drain the soaked dried fruit mixture and combine with the toasted nuts.

Lightly grease 1 cookie sheet.

EGG WASH

1 egg yolk, beaten
2 teaspoons frozen apple
   juice concentrate, at room
   temperature

Punch down the dough. Gradually knead the fruits and nuts into the dough on a well-floured surface, using only as much of the remaining flour as needed to prevent the dough from sticking. Roll the dough into a cylinder 3 inches thick. The roll will be lumpy. Cut in half crosswise. Pinch the cut ends and tuck them under. Place the loaves 3 inches apart on a greased cookie sheet. Let rise, covered with a towel, until doubled, about 1-1/2 hours.

Preheat the oven to 325° F.

Brush the tops and sides of loaves thoroughly with an egg wash made by beating the egg yolk with the apple juice concentrate. Bake for 15 minutes, then brush the loaves again with the egg wash and turn the baking sheet around in oven. Bake for an additional 25 to 30 minutes.

Cool on a baking sheet for 5 minutes before removing to completely cool on a wire rack.

Yield: 2 loaves

Mousses, Whips, & Puddings

C an a mousse become virtuous? Yes, when it is made with low-fat milk or low-fat cream cheese, egg whites, juice concentrates, and fresh fruit. Will you miss the heavy cream and whole eggs? We don't think so – but maybe you should try the Apricot Mousse just to be sure. We think it will make a convert of you.

The recipes in this chapter begin with gelatin-based uncooked desserts and wind up with cooked custards and puddings. Many of them are classics, like the Apple Trifle, which dates back to Victorian England, and Old-Fashioned Rice Pudding, which is as creamy and soothing as any pudding we've ever had.

Sweetening custards with apple juice concentrate is a little tricky as the acids in the juice make the custard sensitive to curdling. It is extremely important not to overheat or overcook these custards. For best results, use a heavy-bottomed saucepan or double boiler set over barely simmering water. Once you begin cooking the custard, stir it constantly over low heat until the first sign of thickening, about 5 to 7 minutes. If lumps appear, use a wire whisk to dissolve them. After cooking for 5 to 7 minutes, you will notice the mixture has thickened just enough to coat a spoon. This is the sign to remove the custard from the heat.

If you aren't sure that your custard is thick enough, take the tip of a second spoon and scrape through the custard clinging to the back of the stirring spoon. The custard is ready to remove from the heat if it does not flow together and close the scrape mark.

If the custard begins to separate and curdle despite your best efforts to cook it gently, quickly lower the bottom of the pan into an ice bath, while whisking the custard to keep it smooth and help it to cool. When it has cooled a little, pour the custard into a bowl, cover the surface with plastic wrap, and chill.

If curdling appears despite your best efforts, press the

custard through a strainer, or immediately whirl the mixture in a blender until smooth. The custard will probably be thinner than it was, but it will taste just fine. If the texture still isn't smooth, discard it.

When to bake a pudding in a hot water bath remains a debatable issue in our minds. The technique may result in a creamier, softer pudding. However, we think our recipes are successful with and without the bath, so we have eliminated it. If you would like to see if you can detect an important difference, do experiment.

Swiss Chocolate Orange Mousse

This is one of those irresistible combinations — chocolate and orange — and it is made in just a few minutes. Serve with the Light Milk Whip (page 210).

1 envelope unflavored gelatin
1 cup low-fat milk
1 ounce unsweetened baking chocolate
1/3 cup frozen apple juice concentrate
1 tablespoon frozen orange juice concentrate
1 tablespoon grated orange rind
1 teaspoon vanilla extract
2 egg whites, at room temperature

In a small bowl, sprinkle the gelatin over the milk. Set aside for 5 minutes.

Melt the chocolate in a small saucepan over very low heat. Stir 2 tablespoons of the milk mixture into the chocolate, using a whisk. Add the remaining milk, a small amount at a time, stirring until the gelatin is dissolved. Flecks of chocolate may remain. Remove from the heat and pour into a bowl. Stir in the apple juice concentrate, orange juice concentrate, orange rind, and vanilla. Chill until the mixture is syrupy.

When the chocolate mixture is ready, beat the egg whites until stiff but not dry. Stir one-quarter of the egg whites into the chocolate mixture, then fold in the rest. Spoon into 6 custard cups or a 1-quart bowl. Serve thoroughly chilled.

Yield: 6 servings

Mango Mousse

The flavor of mangoes blends apricot, nectarine, and peach — with an unexpected hint of tartness. Mangoes are at their peak from mid to late summer. Ask your produce person to select ripe mangoes for you. If none are ready yet, bring them home and wait until they are yellow-red and soft. Mango colors this mousse a lovely delicate orange.

1/2 cup low-fat evaporated milk

2 tablespoons frozen apple juice concentrate, at room temperature

2 tablespoons water

1-1/2 envelopes unflavored gelatin

2 very ripe large mangoes

1 teaspoon lemon juice

1 teaspoon grated orange rind

3 tablespoons frozen apple juice concentrate

Measure the milk into a small mixing bowl and place in the freezer along with the beaters. Chill until ice crystals form around the edge, 20 to 30 minutes.

Combine 2 tablespoons apple juice concentrate with the water. Sprinkle the gelatin over the liquid and let stand for 5 minutes.

Peel the mangoes and scrape the pulp from the fibrous seed. Work over a large bowl to catch all the juice. In a blender or food processor, puree the mangoes with the lemon juice and orange rind until smooth.

In a small saucepan, heat the remaining 3 tablespoons apple juice concentrate until it just begins to boil. Remove from the heat and stir in the softened gelatin until it dissolves. Add to the fruit puree.

Beat the chilled milk with an electric mixer set at the highest speed, beating until fluffy. Fold into the cooked mango mixture. Immediately spoon into 6 dessert dishes or a 1-1/2-quart serving bowl. Serve thoroughly chilled.

Yield: 6 servings

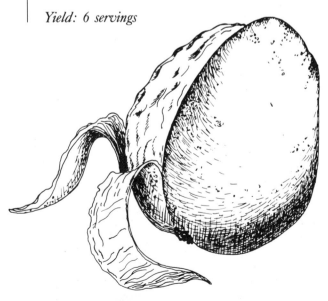

156

Apricot Mousse

If you think mousse means whipping cream, watch what low-fat evaporated milk can do. You must use the high speed of an electric mixer to whip in enough air to transform it into bouffant white peaks. For variety, serve Apricot Mousse in baked tart shells and top with toasted almond bits. Because this recipe calls for dried apricots, it can be a four-season dessert.

1/2 cup low-fat evaporated milk
1/2 cup minced dried apricots (use scissors for mincing)
1/2 teaspoon cinnamon
2 tablespoons frozen apple juice concentrate
1 envelope unflavored gelatin
1/2 cup cold water
1/2 cup frozen apple juice concentrate, at room temperature
1/2 cup orange juice, preferably fresh
1/4 teaspoon almond or rum extract

Measure the milk into a small mixer bowl or narrow deep bowl and place in the freezer along with a beater. Chill until ice crystals form around edge, about 20 to 30 minutes.

Meanwhile, in a small saucepan, combine the apricots, cinnamon, and 2 tablespoons apple juice concentrate. Bring to a boil and remove from the heat.

Combine the gelatin and water in a heatproof cup or bowl and let stand for 5 minutes. Place the container in a pan of simmering water and stir until the gelatin is completely dissolved. Stir into the apricot mixture. Add the remaining 1/2 cup apple juice concentrate, orange juice, and almond or rum extract. Chill, stirring occasionally, until the mixture is syrupy, but not set.

Beat the chilled milk with an electric mixer set at the highest speed, beating until fluffy. Fold into the cooled apricot mixture. Immediately spoon into 6 dessert dishes or a 1-1/2-quart serving bowl. Serve thoroughly chilled.

Yield: 6 servings

Peach Mousse

Make sure your peaches are flavorful and ripe. Substitute unsweetened frozen or canned peaches if necessary.

1 envelope unflavored gelatin
1/2 cup cold water
1/2 cup frozen apple juice
 concentrate
1 teaspoon grated orange
 rind
1/4 cup orange juice,
 preferably fresh
1-1/2 cups sliced, peeled
 peaches (about 4 medium-
 size peaches)
3 ounces low-fat cream
 cheese
1 peach, sliced just before
 serving

In a small bowl, sprinkle the gelatin over the water. Set aside for 5 minutes.

In a saucepan, heat the apple juice concentrate just to boiling. Remove from the heat and stir in the softened gelatin until it is completely dissolved. Pour into a blender along with the orange rind, orange juice, sliced peaches, and cream cheese. Blend until smooth. Pour into 6 dessert dishes or custard cups. Serve thoroughly chilled. Garnish with peach slices.

Yield: 6 servings

Zesty Orange Whip

This fresh and frothy orange gelatin whip will provide a refreshing ending to a rich meal.

1 envelope unflavored gelatin
1/4 cup cold water
2 teaspoons grated orange
 rind
1-3/4 cups fresh orange
 juice
1 cup chopped orange
 segments, drained

Combine the gelatin and water in a heatproof cup or bowl and let stand for 5 minutes. Place the container in a pan of simmering water and stir until the gelatin is completely dissolved.

Measure the orange rind and juice into a bowl. Stir in the dissolved gelatin. Chill until the mixture has a syrupy consistency.

Whip the chilled gelatin until frothy. Fold in the drained orange chunks. Spoon into 4 individual dessert dishes. Serve thoroughly chilled.

Yield: 4 servings

Citrus Berry Pudding

A mint leaf looks festive on top of this rosy pudding. Its tartness is refreshing on a hot summer day.

1 envelope unflavored gelatin
2/3 cup orange juice,
  preferably fresh
1/4 cup frozen apple juice
  concentrate
1 teaspoon grated orange
  rind
1 teaspoon grated lemon rind
1-1/2 cups pureed
  strawberries (fresh or
  unsweetened frozen and
  defrosted)
1/2 cup unsweetened
  applesauce (see page 187)
6 perfect, unstemmed
  strawberries

In a medium-size saucepan, combine the gelatin and orange juice. Let stand for 5 minutes, then stir over low heat until the gelatin is dissolved. Stir in the apple juice concentrate, orange and lemon rinds, pureed strawberries, and applesauce. Pour into 6 custard cups. Top each serving with a strawberry. Serve chilled.

Yield: 6 servings

Orange-Date Pudding

Here's something for tapioca lovers — a spiced fruit pudding you can make in minutes.

1/4 cup quick-cooking tapioca
2-1/4 cups orange juice
  (preferably fresh)
1/4 cup frozen apple juice
  concentrate
1/8 teaspoon allspice
1 cup orange sections
1/2 cup (4 ounces) chopped
  dates, well packed
1/4 cup unsweetened
  shredded coconut

In a small saucepan, combine the tapioca, orange juice, apple juice concentrate, and allspice. Let the mixture stand for 5 minutes.

Bring to a boil over medium heat, stirring constantly. Remove from the heat, transfer to a bowl, and cool for 10 minutes by placing the bowl in the refrigerator or freezer. When the mixture is somewhat cool, stir in the orange sections and dates. Spoon into 6 dessert dishes or a 1-1/2-quart serving bowl. Refrigerate. Serve chilled. Just before serving, sprinkle with coconut.

Yield: 6 servings

Fruited Grape Gelatin

Indulge yourself with your favorite fruit secreted inside a molded grape gelatin. Its glistening regal color will be a highlight on your buffet table.

You can use any fruit in this gelatin, except fresh pineapple, papaya, and kiwi, all of which contain an enzyme that prevents jelling.

1 to 1-1/2 envelopes
  unflavored gelatin
1/4 cup cold water
1-3/4 cups unsweetened
  grape juice
1 to 1-1/2 cups chopped,
  drained, fresh or
  unsweetened frozen and
  defrosted fruits

In a medium-size bowl, sprinkle the gelatin over the water. Use 1 envelope if you plan to serve the dessert in dessert dishes; use 1-1/2 envelopes if you plan to serve it in a mold. Let stand for 5 minutes.

Heat the grape juice until it comes to a boil. Add to the gelatin and stir until dissolved. Chill until the mixture has a syrupy consistency. Fold in the drained fruits. Spoon into dessert dishes or into a 1-1/2-quart mold that has been rinsed in cold water. Chill until firm.

To unmold, run a thin knife between the gelatin and the mold; then dip the mold into hot water for just a second. Invert the mold onto a serving plate.

Yield: 6 servings

Danish Fruit Pudding

The secret of this flavorful pudding is in the exquisite perfume of the berries. Serve with Light Milk Whip (page 210).

1-1/2 cups unsweetened raspberries (fresh or frozen and defrosted)

1-1/2 cups unsweetened sliced strawberries (fresh or frozen and defrosted)

1/2 cup frozen apple juice concentrate

1/4 cup water

2 tablespoons cornstarch

2 tablespoons water

In a saucepan, combine the raspberries, strawberries, apple juice concentrate, and 1/4 cup water. Cook over low heat, stirring occasionally, until the fruit is cooked. Puree in a food processor or blender. Press through a fine sieve to remove any seeds. Return the puree to the saucepan.

Dissolve the cornstarch in the remaining 2 tablespoons water and stir into the berry mixture. Cook over moderate heat, stirring constantly, until thickened. Remove from the heat and spoon into 6 heatproof dessert dishes. Cover and refrigerate. Serve chilled.

Yield: 6 servings

Pineapple-Rice Parfait

A deluxe rice pudding that requires no baking. It is very colorful when topped with Strawberry Sauce (page 204).

2 (20-ounce) cans
  unsweetened crushed
  pineapple, very well-
  drained (with juice pressed
  out and reserved)
1/2 cup (4 ounces) chopped
  dates, well packed
1/2 cup uncooked long-
  grain white rice (not
  converted rice)
2 cups low-fat milk
1 teaspoon vanilla extract
1/2 teaspoon cinnamon
Cinnamon

Combine the crushed pineapple and dates and set aside.

In a medium-size saucepan, bring 1-1/4 cups of the reserved pineapple juice to a boil. Add the rice, cover tightly, and simmer for 20 minutes without removing the lid. Add the milk to the rice mixture and continue to cook, uncovered, over low heat. Stir frequently until the mixture is thick and creamy, about 30 minutes. Remove from the heat. Stir in the vanilla and 1/2 teaspoon cinnamon.

In 6 parfait or sherbet glasses, alternate layers of the rice mixture with the pineapple mixture. Repeat the layers ending with pineapple. Garnish with a dash of cinnamon over each serving. Serve chilled.

Yield: 6 servings

Orange Bavarian Cream in Orange Shells

Using orange shells as serving cups takes time to prepare, but the results are gratifying. The preparation time can be shortened by serving the cream in 8 sherbet glasses or chilling it in a 1-1/2-quart mold.

4 large oranges
2 tablespoons grated orange rind
1/2 cup orange juice
1 envelope unflavored gelatin
2 egg yolks
3/4 cup low-fat milk
1/4 cup frozen apple juice concentrate
3 tablespoons frozen orange juice concentrate
1 teaspoon vanilla extract
2 egg whites, at room temperature
8 mint sprigs

Using a grater, remove just enough rind from both ends of each orange so that ends are flattened and oranges will stand upright. Reserve 2 tablespoons of the grated rind.

Cut the oranges in half crosswise. Squeeze out 1/2 cup of juice. Sprinkle the gelatin over the juice and set aside. Using a grapefruit knife, scoop out the orange sections from the unsqueezed halves. Cut the sections into small chunks to be used as a garnish.

In a small bowl, beat the egg yolks until light in color. Set aside.

Heat the milk in a double-boiler or heavy-bottomed saucepan. When it is hot, stir about 3 tablespoons into the egg yolks, then gradually stir the yolks into the hot milk. Cook over low heat, stirring until slightly thickened. Add the gelatin mixture and stir until dissolved. Remove from the heat. Add the apple juice concentrate, orange juice concentrate, reserved orange rind, and vanilla. Pour the mixture into a bowl. Chill, stirring occasionally, until the mixture is syrupy, but not set.

Beat the egg whites until stiff but not dry. Stir a heaping tablespoon of the whites into the partially jelled mixture. Gently fold in the remainder until combined. Spoon into the orange shells, 8 sherbet glasses, or a 1-1/2-quart mold.

Serve thoroughly chilled. Garnish with orange chunks and mint sprigs.

Yield: 8 servings

Apple Trifle

Trifle, a cherished Victorian invention with an understated name, is an inspired concoction of custard, fruit, and spirit-soaked bread or cake. Show off a trifle by serving it in a cut-glass bowl. The bowl should hold 2 quarts and be at least 8 inches in diameter.

Be sure the bread or cake is at least a day old, dense, and dry so it can soak up the sweet syrup and not become soggy. If need be, "age" the bread or cake by drying it in a moderate oven for a few minutes.

You will need to allow 6 hours for the trifle to chill, or prepare it 1 day ahead.

3 eggs
1/3 cup frozen apple juice concentrate, at room temperature
1-1/2 cups low-fat milk
1 teaspoon vanilla extract
6 to 8 medium-size apples, cored, peeled (optional), and cut into 1/4-inch slices (choose an apple variety that holds its shape when cooked)
1/4 cup frozen apple juice concentrate
1/4 cup water
3 tablespoons frozen apple juice concentrate
3 tablespoons orange juice
1 teaspoon brandy extract
8 to 10 thick slices of day-old bread with crusts removed or 1 layer of stale cake (Birthday Plum Cake, page 24, is recommended)
6 tablespoons unsweetened apple butter (see page 202) or Strawberry Jam (page 203)
Toasted slivered almonds

To make the custard sauce, beat the eggs until thick and lemon-colored in a medium-size bowl. Stir in the 1/3 cup apple juice concentrate. In a heavy saucepan, heat the milk until small bubbles form around the edges of the pan. Stir the hot milk into the egg mixture, a little at a time. Return the sauce to the pan and cook, stirring constantly over very low heat, just until the mixture thickens enough to coat a spoon, about 5 to 7 minutes. It will not be thick. Remove from the heat and stir in the vanilla. Cover the surface of the custard with plastic wrap to prevent a skin from forming and refrigerate.

While the custard cools, place the apple slices in a heavy skillet with the 1/4 cup apple juice concentrate and water. Heat to boiling, cover, reduce the heat, and simmer until the apples are tender, about 8 minutes. Uncover and continue to simmer until the liquid is absorbed. Cool.

Make a fruit syrup by combining the remaining 3 tablespoons apple juice concentrate, orange juice, and brandy extract. Set aside.

To assemble the trifle, use about half the bread to line the bottom of the serving dish. If you are using cake, slice it horizontally into 2 layers and use one layer to line bottom of the bowl. Trim the bread or cake to fit closely together so there are no gaps.

Drizzle half of the fruit syrup over the bread or cake. Spread the apple butter over the bread or cake, then overlap the apple slices on top of the apple butter. Cover with the rest of bread or cake. Drizzle with the remaining fruit syrup. Spoon the custard sauce over the top and help it reach the bottom of the bowl by pulling the trifle gently away from the sides. Refrigerate, covered, for at least 6 hours or overnight.

Just before serving arrange toasted almonds over the top of trifle.

Yield: 6 servings

Old-Fashioned Rice Pudding

This homey dessert deserves its reputation as being satisfying and soothing.

1-1/2 cups unsweetened apple juice (or 1/2 cup frozen apple juice concentrate and 1 cup water)
1/2 cup uncooked long-grain white rice (not converted rice)
2/3 cup raisins
2 eggs
2 cups low-fat milk
1 teaspoon grated lemon rind
1 teaspoon vanilla extract
Ground nutmeg

Preheat the oven to 325° F.

Bring the apple juice to a boil in a medium-size saucepan. Add the rice, cover, and simmer for 15 minutes without removing the lid. Add the raisins and simmer, uncovered, for 5 to 10 minutes longer, or until all the liquid has been absorbed.

In a bowl, beat the eggs lightly. Stir in the milk, lemon rind, and vanilla. Combine with the rice mixture. Use a 1/2 cup measure to transfer to 6 custard cups or a 1-1/2 quart casserole. Sprinkle with nutmeg. Bake until firm, 50 to 60 minutes. Serve warm or chilled.

Yield: 6 servings

Chocolate Rice Pudding

1-1/2 cups unsweetened apple juice (or 1/2 cup frozen apple juice concentrate and 1 cup water)
1/2 cup uncooked long-grain rice (not converted rice)
1/2 cup (4 ounces) finely chopped dates, well packed
3/4 ounce (3/4 square) unsweetened baking chocolate, coarsely chopped
1/4 cup frozen apple juice concentrate, at room temperature
2 eggs
2 cups low-fat milk
1 teaspoon vanilla extract

Preheat the oven to 325° F.

Bring the apple juice to a boil in a medium-size saucepan. Add the rice, cover, and simmer for 15 minutes without removing the lid. Then stir in the dates. Simmer, uncovered, stirring frequently, for 5 minutes, or until the liquid is absorbed. Remove from the heat. Stir in the chocolate.

In a bowl, beat the eggs lightly. Stir in the milk and vanilla. Combine with the rice mixture. Use a 1/2 cup measure to transfer to 6 custard cups or pour into a 1-1/2 quart casserole. Bake until firm, 50 to 60 minutes.

Serve warm or chilled.

Yield: 6 servings

Pineapple Pudding

2 eggs
1-1/2 cups low-fat milk
1/2 cup frozen apple juice concentrate, at room temperature
1 cup (or 20-ounce can) unsweetened crushed pineapple, very well-drained (with juice pressed out)
1 teaspoon vanilla extract
Ground nutmeg

Preheat the oven to 325° F.

In a medium-size bowl, beat the eggs lightly. Add the milk and apple juice concentrate, beating until combined. Stir in the crushed pineapple and vanilla. Use a 1/2-cup measure to transfer the mixture to 6 custard cups or pour into a 1-quart casserole. Sprinkle with nutmeg. Bake for 1 hour or until firm. (The pudding will become firmer as it cools.) Place on a wire rack to cool slightly, then refrigerate. Serve chilled.

Yield: 6 servings

Crunchy Peanut Pudding

This tasty pudding makes an energizing snack. It is good with Light Milk Whip (page 210).

1/2 cup (4 ounces) chopped dates, well packed

1/3 cup frozen apple juice concentrate

1 tablespoon butter or margarine

3 tablespoons unsweetened crunchy or smooth peanut butter

2 egg yolks

2 tablespoons milk

1 teaspoon vanilla extract

1/4 teaspoon nutmeg

3/4 cup coarsely chopped peanuts

1/2 cup dried currants

2 egg whites, at room temperature

1/8 teaspoon cream of tartar

1/8 teaspoon salt (omit if the peanut butter or peanuts are salted)

Preheat the oven to 325° F.

In a small saucepan, combine the dates, apple juice concentrate, and butter. Simmer for about 3 minutes. Puree the mixture in a blender or food processor. Add the peanut butter, egg yolks, milk, vanilla, and nutmeg. Blend until just combined. Transfer to a bowl and stir in the peanuts and currants.

Beat the egg whites until foamy. Add the cream of tartar and salt and continue to beat until stiff, but not dry. Stir one-quarter of the egg whites into the peanut mixture, then gently fold in the rest. Spoon into 6 custard cups. Bake for 15 to 20 minutes or until firm. This is best served warm.

Yield: 6 servings

Bread Pudding

We'll always feel grateful toward the frugal cook who invented this tasty pudding so as not to waste even a crust of bread. It is very easy to make and especially good when served right out of the oven. The flavor will change with your choice of bread — French, whole wheat, white, egg, raisin. Be sure it's old enough, the drier the better.

3 cups cubed dry bread
1/4 cup raisins
1/3 cup (2-1/2 ounces)
   chopped dates, well packed
1 teaspoon cinnamon
1/2 teaspoon nutmeg
2 eggs
1-1/4 cups low-fat milk
1/2 cup frozen apple juice
   concentrate, at room
   temperature
1 teaspoon vanilla extract

Preheat the oven to 350° F. Lightly grease an 8-inch by 8-inch baking pan or 6 custard cups.

In a bowl, combine the bread cubes, raisins, and dates with the cinnamon and nutmeg. Place in the baking pan or distribute in the custard cups.

Beat the eggs lightly. Add the milk, apple juice concentrate, and vanilla. Stir until combined. Pour the mixture over the bread cubes and let it sit for 5 minutes. Bake for 30 to 35 minutes. Serve warm.

Yield: 6 servings

Lemon Custard

Each serving of this lively dessert is topped with a mountain of golden meringue.

CUSTARD

1/2 cup (4 ounces) chopped dates, well packed
2 tablespoons butter or margarine, at room temperature
1/3 cup lemon juice
3 tablespoons grated lemon rind
2 tablespoons frozen apple juice concentrate, at room temperature
1/8 teaspoon salt
3 egg yolks
2 cups low-fat milk
3 tablespoons cornstarch

TOPPING

3 egg whites, at room temperature
1/4 teaspoon cream of tartar
1/8 teaspoon salt
1 tablespoon frozen apple juice concentrate, at room temperature
1 teaspoon grated lemon rind

To make the custard, puree the dates, butter, lemon juice, lemon rind, apple juice concentrate, and salt in a blender or food processor until smooth. Add the egg yolks and milk and continue to blend while adding cornstarch. Transfer the mixture to a heavy saucepan and cook over moderate heat, stirring constantly until thickened, 5 to 7 minutes. Pour into 8 custard cups and refrigerate until cool.

Preheat the oven to 325° F.

When the custard is cool, beat the egg whites until foamy. Add the cream of tartar and salt. Continue beating until the whites are stiff, but not dry. Beat in the apple juice concentrate and lemon rind. Place equal amounts of topping on the cooled custards and bake for 10 minutes or until golden brown. Serve immediately.

Yield: 6 servings

Hot Applesauce Whip

This is applesauce all dressed-up — spiked with spice and topped with an airy meringue. Like a soufflé, it must be served right from the oven.

1-1/2 cups unsweetened
    applesauce (see page 187)
1 tablespoon frozen apple
    juice concentrate
1/2 teaspoon cinnamon
1/4 teaspoon nutmeg
1 teaspoon grated lemon rind
2 tablespoons raisins
4 egg whites, at room
    temperature
Cinnamon

Preheat the oven to 350° F. Lightly grease 6 custard cups. Put the applesauce into a strainer to drain off any excess liquid.

Blend the applesauce with the apple juice concentrate, cinnamon, nutmeg, and lemon rind. Spoon 1-1/2 tablespoons of the mixture into the bottom of each of the custard cups. Sprinkle each portion with a few raisins.

Beat the egg whites until stiff, but not dry. Very gently fold the whites into the remaining applesauce. Spoon into the cups and sprinkle the tops with cinnamon. Bake for 15 to 20 minutes, until puffed and golden. Serve immediately.

Yield: 6 servings

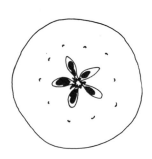  

Prune Whip

The sweet, winey resonance of prunes is delicately presented in this old-fashioned dessert.

3/4 cup chopped prunes,
  well packed
1/3 cup frozen apple juice
  concentrate
1/4 cup water
1 tablespoon unbleached
  white flour
2 tablespoons grated lemon
  rind
1 tablespoon lemon juice
1/4 teaspoon allspice
4 egg whites, at room
  temperature
1/4 teaspoon cream
  of tartar
1/8 teaspoon salt

Preheat the oven to 300° F.

Simmer the prunes in the apple juice concentrate and water until about 2 tablespoons of liquid remains. Remove from the heat and puree in a blender or food processor with the flour, lemon rind, lemon juice, and allspice until well combined. Transfer to a large bowl and cool to room temperature.

Beat the egg whites until foamy. Add the cream of tartar and salt and continue to beat until stiff but not dry. Stir one-quarter of the egg whites into the prune mixture, then gently fold in the rest. Spoon into a 1-1/2-quart soufflé dish or 6 custard cups. Bake for 30 minutes in the soufflé dish and 20 minutes in the custard cups. Serve immediately.

Yield: 6 servings

Pineapple Pudding Cake

As this pudding bakes, a golden, cake-like layer rises and covers the creamy pineapple custard below. Peaches or apricots can be used in place of the pineapple.

1 cup (20-ounce can) unsweetened crushed pineapple, very well-drained (with juice pressed out)
3 egg yolks
1 teaspoon grated lemon rind
1 teaspoon grated orange rind
3 tablespoons flour
1 cup low-fat milk
1 teaspoon vanilla extract
3 tablespoons frozen apple juice concentrate, at room temperature
3 tablespoons frozen orange juice concentrate, at room temperature
3 egg whites, at room temperature
1/8 teaspoon cream of tartar
1/8 teaspoon salt

Preheat the oven to 300° F. Spoon equal amounts of the crushed pineapple into 8 custard cups.

In a medium-size bowl, beat the egg yolks until thick and lemon-colored. Blend in the lemon and orange rinds. Add the milk alternately with the flour, stirring until well-blended. Stir in the vanilla and fruit juice concentrates.

Beat the egg whites until foamy. Add the cream of tartar and salt and continue to beat until stiff but not dry. Stir one-quarter of the egg whites into the batter, then gently fold in the rest. Spoon the mixture over the crushed pineapple. Bake for 35 to 40 minutes. Serve warm or cold.

Yield: 8 servings

Simple Fruit Desserts & Ices

W hen it comes to simple fruit desserts, virtue is hardly a factor. We simply enjoy eating desserts where the flavor of fruit is allowed to stand out, uncomplicated by heavy batters and creams.

Besides being low in calories, these simple desserts have the added advantage of being exceptionally easy and quick to prepare. In many cases, such as Fresh Fruit Ambrosia and the Patriot's Pudding, no cooking is necessary. In other desserts, such as the Baked Fresh Fruit Compote and the Tahitian Bananas, only the briefest cooking or baking is required. These are all recipes that celebrate fresh fruits in season.

Several of the recipes in this chapter are for frozen desserts – sherbets, ices, yogurt, and the like. The recipes have instructions for making these desserts by the still-freezing method, without the aid of an ice cream maker. However, if you do have an ice cream maker, you will find it makes a smoother dessert. Just follow the manufacturer's directions.

The recipes have been tested in a separate freezer unit that is set at 0° F. If you are going to make frozen desserts using the freezer compartment of a refrigerator, you may need to move the temperature control to the coldest setting in order to reach a sufficiently cold temperature.

These frozen desserts tend to freeze solid if they are not used within a few hours after they are made. You can make these desserts ahead of time and then allow the mixture to soften at room temperature for about 15 minutes. Beat vigorously with an electric beater or a hand whisk until the softened dessert is smooth but not melted. Serve at once, store in the refrigerator for 15 minutes, or return to the freezer for 30 minutes. You can repeat this process again and again if you have leftovers (which is doubtful). When tightly covered, frozen desserts will keep in the freezer for about a month. If a frozen dessert is kept too long the flavor dissipates. To refresh a frozen dessert, let it soften and then whip in some fresh fruit or juice and refreeze.

Frozen fruit frosts are especially wonderful frozen desserts because you need only two things to make them: a food processor and frozen fruit. Almost any fresh fruit will do, as long it has been frozen. You simply puree the frozen fruit with a little flavoring in a food processor and you have an incredibly refreshing drink for a hot summer evening. If the frost is not served immediately, cover it tightly and store it in the freezer. When you are ready to serve, let it sit for 15 minutes at room temperature to soften. Give it another whirl in the food processor if necessary.

Fresh Fruit Ambrosia

There are endless variations on ambrosia desserts. Ours combines fresh fruits with yogurt, nuts, and toasted coconut. It is an excellent accompaniment to the substantial platters on a festive buffet table.

2 apples, diced
2 oranges, peeled and cut
   into segments
2 bananas, sliced
1 cup seeded and halved
   red grapes or cherries
1 cup seedless green grapes
2/3 cup (5 ounces) chopped
   dates, well packed
2 teaspoons grated orange
   rind
2 tablespoons frozen apple
   juice concentrate
2/3 cup toasted sunflower
   seeds or chopped walnuts
2/3 cup toasted unsweetened
   shredded coconut
2 to 3 cups plain nonfat
   yogurt

Combine the apples, oranges, bananas, red grapes or cherries, green grapes, and dates with the orange rind and apple juice concentrate.

About 15 minutes before serving, add the seeds, nuts, coconut, and yogurt to the fruit. Stir to combine. Cover and refrigerate to allow the flavors to meld. This can be held in the refrigerator for up to 1 hour. Serve chilled.

Yield: 8 servings

Patriot's Pudding

An astonishingly colorful dessert that takes no time at all to make.

2 cups ricotta cheese
1/2 teaspoon grated orange
  rind
2 teaspoons frozen apple
  juice concentrate, at room
  temperature
1-1/2 cups fresh blueberries
1-1/2 cups fresh raspberries
  or strawberries

Mix the ricotta cheese with the lemon rind and apple juice concentrate.

Rinse the berries and pat them dry. Slice the strawberries.

Make a layer of ricotta cheese in each of 6 dessert or sherbet glasses. Arrange the blueberries and raspberries or strawberries alternately with layers of cheese until the glasses are filled. Serve thoroughly chilled.

Yield: 6 servings

Apple-Prune Royale

Prunes give a robust undertone to this attractively arranged dessert. Its full-bodied sweetness is perfect for the winter months when fresh summer fruits aren't available.

1-1/2 cups pitted prunes
1 cup unsweetened grape juice
Whole blanched almonds
2 tablespoons frozen apple
  juice concentrate
4 apples, peeled, cored, and
  sliced 1/4 inch thick
1 lemon, thinly sliced
1 tablespoon butter
1 teaspoon cinnamon
1/2 teaspoon nutmeg
1 teaspoon grated orange rind

Soak the prunes in the grape juice overnight. Drain and reserve the juice. Stuff each prune with an almond.

Preheat the oven to 350° F.

In a skillet, heat the apple juice concentrate; add the apples and lemon slices and sauté for 2 minutes. Spoon the apples in a ring around the outside edge of 1-quart round casserole. Fill the center with the stuffed prunes.

In a small saucepan, melt the butter and combine with the cinnamon, nutmeg, orange rind, and reserved grape juice. Heat the mixture thoroughly and pour over the fruit. Bake for 15 minutes. Serve warm or chilled.

Yield: 6 servings

Mountain Berry Meringue

This is a simple but impressive dessert. The fruit is steeped in orange juice and then given a cloud-like cover of beaten egg whites and baked in the oven until golden.

FRUIT

6 cups (1-1/2 quarts) fresh
  or frozen strawberries (or
  other berries), sliced
2 tablespoons frozen apple
  juice concentrate, at room
  temperature
2 teaspoons grated orange
  rind
3 tablespoons orange juice

TOPPING

4 egg whites, at room
  temperature
1/4 teaspoon cream
  of tartar
1/8 teaspoon salt
2 tablespoons frozen apple
  juice concentrate, at room
  temperature
1 teaspoon grated orange
  rind
3 tablespoons slivered
  almonds

Place the strawberries in a shallow 2-quart or 3-quart baking dish. Combine the apple juice concentrate, orange rind, and orange juice and pour over the fruit. Let stand for 30 to 60 minutes.

Just before serving, preheat the oven to 400° F. and prepare the topping. Beat the egg whites until foamy. Add the cream of tartar and salt and continue to beat until the whites are stiff but not dry. Beat in the apple juice concentrate and orange rind. Spoon mounds of the meringue over the fruit. Sprinkle with the almonds. Bake for 4 to 5 minutes, or until the top begins to brown. Serve immediately. Spoon some of the fruit juice over each portion.

Yield: 6 servings

Strawberry-Blueberry Rhubarb

Serve for dessert with a plate of cookies.

4 cups rhubarb, cut into
   1-inch pieces (peel stalks
   if the rhubarb is stringy)
1/2 cup frozen apple juice
   concentrate
1 pint strawberries, halved
1 cup blueberries

In a medium-size (nonaluminum) saucepan, combine the rhubarb and apple juice concentrate. Bring to a boil, then reduce the heat. Simmer, covered, for 5 minutes. Add the strawberries, cover, and simmer for 3 to 4 minutes, or until the strawberries are slightly transparent. Stir in the blueberries and simmer for 1 minute longer. Serve warm or chilled.

Yield: 6 to 8 servings

Baked Fresh Fruit Compote

This medley of sweet fruit flavors is accented with a light touch of spice and whole almonds. For variety, replace the cinnamon stick and cloves with 1 tablespoon finely chopped Glazed Ginger Root (page 207).

1/2 cup orange juice
1/2 cup pineapple juice
2 tablespoons frozen apple
   juice concentrate
1/2 lemon, thinly sliced
1 cinnamon stick
2 whole cloves
Pinch salt
1 teaspoon orange rind
3 large baking apples, sliced
   1 to 2 inches thick
2 large pears, quartered
Lemon juice
2 bananas, quartered
3/4 cup seeded, halved dark
   grapes or pitted black
   cherries
1/4 cup toasted almonds

Preheat the oven to 350° F. Lightly grease a 2-quart casserole with lid.

In a saucepan, combine the orange and pineapple juices, apple juice concentrate, lemon, cinnamon, cloves, salt, and orange rind. Bring to a boil and stir constantly for 1 minute; remove from the heat.

Place the apple and pears in the casserole dish. Sprinkle with the lemon juice to prevent discoloring. Pour the orange-pineapple juice over the fruits. Bake for 20 minutes.

Sprinkle the bananas with a little more lemon juice, then add to the baking dish along with the grapes. Gently push the fruits into the cooking syrup, cover loosely, and bake for 10 minutes longer.

Sprinkle almonds over each serving. Serve hot or cold.

Yield: 4 to 6 servings

Tahitian Bananas

Serve this simple banana sensation right out of the oven. If you like, sprinkle each serving with finely chopped roasted peanuts.

4 firm ripe bananas, halved
   lengthwise
Juice of 1 lime
3/4 cup orange juice,
   preferably fresh
1/4 cup frozen apple juice
   concentrate
1/2 teaspoon ground ginger
1/4 teaspoon nutmeg
1/4 teaspoon cinnamon
2 teaspoons rum extract
1 tablespoon butter
Nutmeg

Lightly grease a 13-inch by 9-inch baking pan. Preheat the oven to 450° F.

Place the bananas cut side down in the prepared baking dish. Brush with the lime juice.

In a small saucepan, combine the orange juice, apple juice concentrate, ginger, 1/4 teaspoon nutmeg, and cinnamon. Bring to a boil, then simmer for 1 minute. Remove from the heat and stir in the rum extract. Pour over the bananas. Dot with the butter. Bake for 10 to 15 minutes, or until the bananas are tender, basting once or twice.

Sprinkle with nutmeg and serve immediately.

Yield: 4 servings

Glazed Oranges

Peeled oranges are sliced, then stacked back together, served in a pool of their own tangy juices and crowned with sparkling strips of peel. For the oranges, navels are a good choice.

6 large oranges
1/4 cup frozen apple juice
   concentrate
3/4 cup orange juice or
   unsweetened pineapple
   juice
Mint leaves

With a vegetable peeler, remove just the orange part of the peel from 3 of the oranges. Cut the peel into very fine strips.

Place the strips in a small saucepan, cover with water, and boil for 5 minutes. Drain, cover with fresh water and repeat the process. Drain and add the apple juice concentrate to the peel in the saucepan. Bring to a boil, cooking rapidly until the liquid is absorbed and the peel is glazed. Set aside.

Peel the remaining 3 oranges (leaving the white membrane if desired). Cut all 6 oranges in 1/4-inch slices. Stack the slices and reshape the oranges into their original form, holding them together with toothpicks. Place in 6 dessert dishes. Pour a portion of the orange or pineapple juice over each orange. Sprinkle with the glazed strips. Garnish with the mint leaves. Refrigerate for at least 1 hour before serving.

Yield: 6 servings

Orange Poached Pears

These will melt in your mouth. A sprinkling of glazed orange peel adds a zesty garnish.

Peel of 2 oranges
2 tablespoons frozen apple
 juice concentrate
6 large pears (of uniform
 ripeness)
Juice of 1 lemon
Juice of 2 oranges plus
 additional orange juice to
 make 2-1/2 cups
2-1/2 cups apple juice (or
 1/2 cup frozen apple juice
 concentrate and 2 cups
 water)
1/2 teaspoon vanilla extract
3-inch piece cinnamon stick
2/3 cup golden raisins

With a vegetable peeler, remove the orange part of the peel from 2 oranges in strips. Scrape off any white residue from the underside of the peel. Cut the peel into very fine strips. Reserve the oranges for juice.

In a very small saucepan, blanch the strips in boiling water for 5 minutes. Drain, cover with fresh water and repeat the process. Drain, add the frozen apple juice concentrate, and simmer over low heat, stirring until all the liquid is absorbed. Set aside.

Peel the pears. To prevent the pears from darkening, brush them with lemon juice or drop into water containing a little lemon juice. In a small Dutch oven or saucepan that will hold the pears upright, combine the orange juice, apple juice, vanilla, cinnamon stick, and raisins. Add the pears and heat to boiling; reduce the heat and simmer for 20 to 25 minutes or until the pears are tender when pierced with the tip of a sharp knife. Cool slightly, then transfer to 2-quart serving bowl. Pour the poaching liquid over the pears. Serve or refrigerate until chilled.

Serve in dessert dishes with some of the poaching liquid spooned on the pears. Arrange the orange strips over the top.

Yield: 6 servings

Summer Pudding

The 18th-century English invented this pudding for those who could no longer tolerate the excessively rich pastries so fashionable at the time. It requires no baking but should be made well ahead of time because it needs to chill for at least 8 hours. Serve with Light Milk Whip (page 210).

8 to 10 slices stale white or whole wheat bread

2-1/4 cups (12 ounces) blueberries (fresh or unsweetened frozen and defrosted fruit)

2-1/4 cups (12 ounces) strawberries (fresh or unsweetened frozen and defrosted fruit)

1 cooking apple, coarsely chopped

2 teaspoons grated orange rind

1/2 teaspoon cinnamon

1/2 cup frozen apple juice concentrate

Finely grated orange rind

Line a 1-quart serving bowl with plastic wrap.

Remove the crusts from the bread. Using as many slices as needed, completely line the bottom and sides of the bowl. Trim the slices to fit closely together, leaving no gaps. Reserve the remaining slices for the top.

Drain the berries and place in a wide, heavy-bottomed pan. Add the chopped apple and sprinkle with the 2 teaspoons orange rind and cinnamon. Add the apple juice concentrate. Bring to a boil over very low heat and cook only until the juices have begun to run. Using a slotted spoon, fill the bread-lined dish with the fruit. Reserve the remaining juice. Completely cover the fruit with additional bread slices. Put a plate that fits inside of the dish on top of the pudding and weight it down with a heavy object. Refrigerate for at least 8 hours.

Before serving, uncover the pudding and unmold it by turning it upside down onto a serving plate. Pour the remaining fruit juices over the top and along the sides of pudding. The juice will tint the surface of the bread with a lovely berry color. Sprinkle grated orange rind over the top. Cut into wedges to serve.

Yield: 6 servings

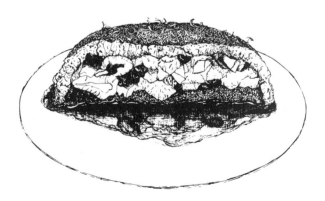

Baked Apples with an Orange Twist

Baked apples are plain fare, but this is a luxurious version.

4 baking apples
1/2 lemon
4 to 6 dates, pitted and
   quartered
1 heaping tablespoon raisins
1/4 cup chopped almonds
2 large oranges
Apple Juice

Preheat the oven to 350° F.

Core the apples, stopping 1/2 inch from the bottom. Pare a 1-inch strip of skin from around the top. Rub the cut surfaces with lemon, dribbling a few drops into the cores. Arrange the apples in a baking dish just large enough to hold them comfortably. Fill the cores with the dates, raisins, and nuts.

With a vegetable peeler, remove just the orange part of the orange peel. Cut the peel into very fine strips. Juice the oranges and measure the juice. Add an equal quantity of apple juice, or enough to make about 1/2 inch of juice in the bottom of the baking dish. Pour the juice around apples. Drop the cut strips of orange peel into the juices.

Bake, basting with the juices every 10 minutes, for 50 minutes, or until the apples are tender when pierced with a knife. They should be soft inside but still hold their shape. The juices at bottom of dish should be slightly thickened. If not, pour into a small pan with the orange strips, simmer, and reduce the liquid until it is thickened and the strips are glazed. Spoon the mixture over the apples. Serve warm.

Yield: 4 servings

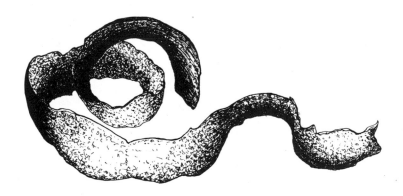

Gingered Peaches

Peaches are even more succulent when they are infused with the bite of fresh ginger. Serve after an Indian dinner.

6 ripe freestone peaches,
   peeled or unpeeled
Juice of 1/2 lemon
1/2 cup chopped almonds
1 tablespoon grated fresh
   ginger root
1/2 cup (4 ounces) finely
   chopped dates, well packed
Unsweetened pineapple juice

Preheat the oven to 350° F. Lightly grease an 11-inch by 7-inch baking dish.

Halve the peaches and sprinkle with the lemon juice. Using a melon baller or spoon, slightly deepen the pit cavity.

In a food processor or blender, process the almonds with the ginger and dates until finely ground. Mound the cavity of each peach half with a portion of the mixture. Pour the pineapple juice over and around the peaches. Bake for 30 minutes or until tender, basting occasionally. Serve warm or chilled with the juices.

Yield: 6 servings

Applesweet Applesauce

Take advantage of the fall harvest when apples are at their best to freeze a quantity of this cinnamon-scented applesauce to enjoy later on pancakes or warm gingerbread. One cup of stewed fruit (such as apricots, cranberries, rhubarb, or strawberries) can be added to the applesauce to give even more flavor and texture.

5 or 6 apples (Golden
   Delicious preferred), peeled
   (optional), cored, and
   chopped
1 cup apple juice (or 1/4
   cup frozen apple juice
   concentrate and 3/4 cup
   water)
1 teaspoon cinnamon
2 teaspoons lemon or
   orange rind
Lemon juice to taste

In a small saucepan, combine the apples with the apple juice concentrate and water. Heat to boiling, then cover and simmer until the apples are very soft. For chunky style applesauce, uncover and mash the apples with a fork. If you prefer a smoother applesauce, blend, strain, or puree the mixture. Continue to simmer until the liquid is absorbed. Add cinnamon, lemon or orange rind, and lemon juice to taste. Serve warm or chilled.

Note: To stew fruits, cover the fruit with apple juice and simmer until softened. Additional frozen apple juice concentrate may be needed if the fruit is tart. Drain before adding to the applesauce.

Yield: Approximately 2 cups

Frozen Persimmons

Contained in its own skin, a frozen persimmon makes an unusual dessert. Select soft, ripe, unblemished fruit with stem caps still attached. Allow 4 to 5 hours for freezing the fruit. This recipe makes 1 serving; multiply the recipe as needed.

1 persimmon
2 teaspoons frozen apple
  juice concentrate
1/2 teaspoon lemon juice
Cinnamon

Place the persimmons on a pie plate or small tray, standing them stem-side down. Freeze, uncovered, until solid, 4 to 5 hours. (For longer freezing, wrap individually in foil and freeze for up to 2 weeks.)

About 1 to 1 1/2 hours before serving, transfer the frozen persimmons to the refrigerator to partially thaw, only until the pulp is semi-frozen.

At serving time, remove the top of each persimmon with a sharp knife and place each fruit in a dessert dish. Make a glaze by combining the apple juice concentrate with the lemon juice. Spoon a little glaze mixture over each fruit. Sprinkle with cinnamon. The pulp should be eaten right out of the skin with a spoon.

Yield: 1 serving

Pineapple Freeze

If you like, substitute your favorite fruits and juices for the pineapple in this recipe.

1 (20-ounce) can
  unsweetened crushed
  pineapple with juice (or
  2 cups fruit of your choice)
Additional unsweetened
  fruit juices (pineapple,
  apple, orange)
1 package unflavored gelatin
Slivers of orange rind

Drain the juice from the pineapple into a large measuring cup. Add additional fruit juice to make a total of 2-1/2 cups juice. Pour 1/2 cup of the juice into a medium-sized saucepan. Sprinkle the gelatin over it. Let stand for 5 minutes.

Add the remaining juice to the saucepan and bring to a boil. Stir into the gelatin until it is completely dissolved. Add the crushed pineapple and pour into an 8-inch metal pan or bowl. Freeze until firm.

Remove from the freezer and beat vigorously with a

whisk or electric beater until foamy but not melted. Cover and freeze until firm. Remove from the freezer 15 minutes before serving to soften. Beat again for a smoother consistency.

Garnish with slivers of orange rind on each serving.

Yield: 1 quart

Frozen Nesselrode Pudding

We have Count Nesselrode, a 19th-century Russian diplomat, to thank for this recipe. It was his chef who brought forth the original Nesselrode pudding. Our version is chock-full of chewy apricots and raisins and flavored with rum extract.

1/3 cup finely chopped
   dried apricots
1 cup raisins
1/2 cup frozen apple juice
   concentrate, heated just to
   boiling
2 eggs or 4 egg yolks
1/8 teaspoon salt
1-1/2 cups scalded milk
1 teaspoon grated orange rind
1 teaspoon rum extract
1 cup milk

In a bowl, soak the apricots and raisins in the hot apple juice concentrate for several hours or overnight.

Lightly beat the eggs and salt together, then gradually stir in 2 to 3 tablespoons of the scalded milk. Add the remaining scalded milk in a steady stream, stirring constantly. Transfer the mixture to a heavy saucepan and cook, stirring constantly, until the mixture thickens enough to coat a spoon, 5 to 7 minutes. Pour into an 8-inch metal pan or bowl, cover, and refrigerate until thoroughly chilled.

Stir in the orange rind, rum extract, 1 cup milk, and soaked fruit and juice. Freeze until solid around the edge and mushy in the center.

Remove from the freezer and beat vigorously with a whisk or electric beater until creamy but not melted. Cover and freeze until firm. Remove from the freezer 15 minutes before serving to soften. Beat again for a smoother consistency.

Yield: 1 quart

Minted Pineapple Frost

You can whip up a frost in an instant with a food processor.

2 (20-ounce) cans
   unsweetened pineapple
   slices
1 tablespoon fresh mint
   leaves or 1 teaspoon dried

Drain the pineapple and reserve 2/3 cup of the juice.

Arrange the pineapple slices in a single layer on a baking sheet. Freeze until solid. Just before serving, use a wide spatula to slide the fruit off pan. Break the slices into small pieces and put immediately into a food processor. Add the reserved pineapple juice and mint leaves. Puree for about 5 minutes, scraping down the sides of the bowl until the mixture is smooth but not melted. Serve immediately.

Yield: 4 cups

Black Cherry Frost

1 pound unsweetened pitted
   black cherries, frozen
Grated rind of 1 orange
1/3 cup orange juice,
   preferably fresh
1 teaspoon brandy extract

Just before serving, place the frozen cherries, orange rind, orange juice, and brandy extract in a food processor. Puree for 30 to 60 seconds, scraping down the sides of bowl until the mixture is smooth but not melted. Serve immediately.

Yield: 3 cups

Peach Frost

6 ripe peaches or
  nectarines, peeled
1 teaspoon lemon juice
1 tablespoon orange juice

Pit the fruit and cut into 1/2-inch slices. Sprinkle with the lemon juice and arrange slightly apart in a single layer on a baking sheet. Freeze until solid. Just before serving, use a wide spatula to slide the fruit off the pan. Put immediately into a food processor with the orange juice. Puree for 30 to 60 seconds, scraping down the sides of the bowl until the mixture is smooth but not melted. Serve immediately.

Yield: 3 cups

Pink Grapefruit Ice

This pleasantly tart refresher with its subtle pink blush looks elegant garnished with a mint leaf or a fresh berry.

2 teaspoons unflavored gelatin
2 tablespoons cold water
1-1/2 cups unsweetened
  pink grapefruit juice (1
  large grapefruit yields 3/4
  to 1 cup juice)
2/3 cup frozen apple juice
  concentrate, at room
  temperature
1 egg white, at room
  temperature

Combine the gelatin and water in a heatproof cup or bowl and let stand for 5 minutes. Place the container in a pan of simmering water and stir until the gelatin is completely dissolved.

Pour the grapefruit juice and apple juice concentrate into an 8-inch metal pan or bowl. Stir in the dissolved gelatin. Freeze until the mixture is solid around the edges but the center is still mushy.

Remove from the freezer and beat vigorously with a whisk or electric beater until foamy but not melted. Beat the egg white until soft peaks form. Fold into the frozen mixture. (The egg white may separate, but it will combine in final beating.) Cover and freeze until firm. Remove from freezer 15 minutes before serving to soften. Beat again for a smoother consistency.

Yield: 2-1/2 cups

Pear Ice

Choose pears that are fully ripened and flavorful. Serve Pear Ice for dessert garnished with toasted almonds. It also makes a wonderful palate cleanser to serve between courses. Offer small portions and omit the garnish.

2 teaspoons unflavored gelatin
2 tablespoons cold water
4 large firm ripe pears, peeled and thinly sliced
1/2 cup frozen apple juice concentrate
1/2 cup water
1/2 teaspoon grated lemon rind
2 teaspoons lemon juice
Sliced fresh pears
Toasted slivered almonds

Sprinkle the gelatin over the 2 tablespoons water and let stand for 5 minutes.

In a small saucepan, combine the pears, apple juice concentrate, remaining 1/2 cup water, lemon rind, and lemon juice. Bring to a boil, cover, reduce the heat, and simmer for 5 to 8 minutes, or until the pears are tender. Remove from the heat and pour into a blender or food processor. Add the gelatin mixture. Whirl until pureed. Pour into an 8-inch metal pan or bowl. Freeze until solid around the edge and mushy in the center.

Remove from the freezer and beat vigorously with a whisk or electric beater until foamy but not melted. Cover and freeze until firm. Remove from the freezer 15 minutes before serving to soften. Beat again for a smoother consistency.

Garnish individual servings with pear slices and toasted almonds.

Yield: 2-1/2 to 3 cups

Watermelon Ice

This frosty pastel pink ice makes a refreshing ending to a summer supper. For a special presentation, serve in a small, hollowed-out watermelon half. Garnish with blueberries and strawberries.

2 teaspoons unflavored gelatin
2 tablespoons cold water
3 cups finely diced seeded
   watermelon
1 tablespoon lemon juice
1/4 cup frozen apple juice
   concentrate
1 egg white, at room
   temperature
Pinch salt

Combine the gelatin and water in a heatproof cup or bowl and let stand for 5 minutes. Place the container in a pan of simmering water and stir until the gelatin is completely dissolved.

Puree the watermelon with the lemon juice and apple juice concentrate in a blender or food processor. Pour into an 8-inch metal pan or bowl. Stir in the dissolved gelatin. Freeze until the mixture is solid around the edge and mushy in the center.

Remove from the freezer and beat vigorously with a whisk or electric beater until foamy but not melted. Beat the egg white and salt until soft peaks form. Fold into the frozen mixture. (The egg white may separate but will combine in final beating.) Cover and freeze until firm. Remove from the freezer 15 minutes before serving to soften. Beat again for a smoother consistency.

Yield: 3 cups

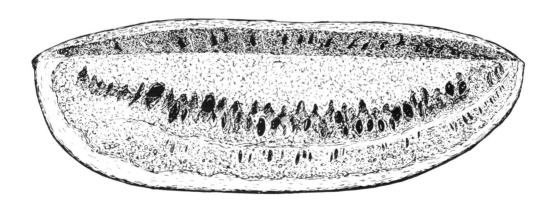

Nutty Banana Ice Milk

A crunchy frozen dessert with a banana flavor that is popular with children.

1-1/2 teaspoons unflavored
  gelatin
1/2 cup fresh orange juice
1-1/2 cups mashed ripe
  bananas (about 3 large
  bananas)
1/3 cup frozen apple juice
  concentrate
1-1/4 cups low-fat
  evaporated milk
1 teaspoon vanilla extract
1 teaspoon grated orange
  rind
2 egg whites, at room
  temperature
1/2 cup chopped walnuts

Combine the gelatin and orange juice in a heatproof cup or bowl and let stand for 5 minutes. Place the container in a pan of simmering water and stir until the gelatin is completely dissolved.

Puree the bananas and apple juice concentrate in a blender or food processor. Blend in the evaporated milk, vanilla, and orange rind. Transfer to a large bowl. Stir in the dissolved gelatin.

Beat the egg whites until stiff but not dry. Fold into the banana mixture. Pour into an 8-inch metal pan or bowl. Freeze until solid around the edge and mushy in the center.

Remove from the freezer and beat vigorously with a whisk or electric beater until creamy but not melted. Fold in the chopped nuts. Cover and freeze until firm. Remove from freezer 15 minutes before serving to soften. Beat again for a smoother consistency.

Yield: 1 quart

Frozen Strawberry Yogurt

You will be tempted to have seconds of this full-bodied, strawberry-scented blend.

1 envelope unflavored gelatin
1/2 cup low-fat evaporated
   milk
2 cups halved strawberries
   (fresh or unsweetened
   frozen)
3/4 cup frozen apple juice
   concentrate
1-1/2 cups plain nonfat yogurt
2 egg whites, at room
   temperature
1/4 cup frozen apple juice
   concentrate, at room
   temperature
Fresh strawberries

Combine the gelatin and milk in a heatproof cup or bowl and let the mixture stand for 5 minutes. Place the container in a pan of simmering water and stir until the gelatin is dissolved.

In a saucepan, heat the strawberries and 3/4 cup apple juice concentrate. Bring to a boil, reduce the heat, and simmer for 5 minutes. Remove from the heat. Stir in the gelatin mixture. Cool slightly. Blend in the yogurt. Transfer to a large bowl.

Beat the egg whites until stiff but not dry. Gradually add the remaining 1/4 cup apple juice concentrate, beating continuously until it is incorporated. Fold into the strawberry mixture. Pour into an 8-inch metal pan or bowl. Freeze until solid around the edge and mushy in the center.

Remove from the freezer and beat vigorously with a whisk or electric beater until creamy but not melted. Cover and freeze until firm. Remove from the freezer 15 minutes before serving to soften. Beat again for a smoother consistency.

Arrange fresh strawberries on each serving.

Yield: 1 quart

Frozen Peach Velvet

This creamy, mousse-like frozen dessert is made quickly in the blender.

5 to 6 medium-size
   peaches, peeled, or 2-1/2
   cups sliced peaches
   (unsweetened canned or
   frozen and defrosted)
1/4 teaspoon almond extract
2/3 cup frozen apple juice
   concentrate
1/2 cup plain nonfat yogurt
1/2 cup low-fat sour cream
1 peach

Slice and pit the 5 to 6 peaches. Place in a blender or food processor with the almond extract, apple juice concentrate, yogurt, and sour cream. Blend until smooth. Pour into an 8-inch metal pan or bowl. Freeze until solid around the edge and mushy in the center.

Remove from the freezer and beat vigorously with a whisk or electric beater until creamy but not melted. Cover and freeze until firm. Remove from the freezer 15 minutes before serving to soften. Beat again for a smoother consistency.

Just before serving peel and slice the remaining peach. Arrange the peach slices on each serving.

Yield: 3-1/2 to 4 cups

Tangy Banana Sherbet

Remarkably easy to make, this delicious sherbet can be enjoyed immediately, without freezing, as a refreshing, frothy drink.

4 ripe bananas
1 (20-ounce) can
   unsweetened, crushed
   pineapple with juice
1/2 cup frozen orange juice
   concentrate
1 teaspoon grated orange rind
1/2 cup nonfat dry milk
   powder

Place all the ingredients in a food processor or blender. Blend until smooth. Pour into an 8-inch metal pan or bowl. Freeze until firm.

Remove from the freezer and process in a food processor or beat with an electric mixer until the mixture is foamy but not melted. Cover and freeze until firm. Remove from the freezer 15 minutes before serving to soften. Beat again for a smoother consistency.

Yield: 3 cups

Creamy Fruit Sherbet

This sherbet calls for frozen milk cubes and chunks of frozen fruits. It is made with the help of either a food processor or the combination of a blender and electric mixer. For variety, try Creamy Fruit Sherbet with yogurt in place of milk, or celebrate a warm summer's night and serve it soft with a straw as a shake.

1 cup low-fat milk
1 to 1-1/2 cups fresh or
  frozen fruit
1/2 cup frozen apple juice
  concentrate
1 teaspoon grated orange rind
Strips of orange or lemon rind

Pour the milk into an ice cube tray and freeze. Cut the fresh fruits into chunks and freeze. Keep already frozen fruits in the freezer.

Shortly before serving, if you are using a food processor, remove the milk and fruit from the freezer. Let stand a few minutes to soften. Chop the cubes if they are large. Whirl the frozen milk pieces, one third at a time, using on-off bursts. When the ice is broken up, add the apple juice concentrate and orange rind and process continuously until velvety. Add the fruit, one third at a time, and process until smooth.

If you are using a blender and electric mixer, remove the milk and fruit from freezer. In the blender, puree the fruit with the apple juice concentrate and orange rind. Set aside. Place the milk cubes in a mixing bowl and break into pieces using a wooden spoon. Using the mixer, beat until smooth, slowly at first, then with increasing speed. Beat in the fruit puree.

If the texture is too soft, cover and place in the freezer until the desired firmness is reached. Garnish each serving with strips of orange or lemon rind.

Freeze leftover sherbet but allow to soften before serving. Beat again for a smoother consistency.

Yield: 3 cups

Date Sherbet

Chewy dates, smooth banana, and creamy yogurt blend deliciously in this unusual sherbet.

3/4 cup (6 ounces) chopped
   dates, well packed
1/2 cup orange juice
1/2 cup apple juice
2 teaspoons lemon juice
2 ripe bananas
1 cup plain nonfat yogurt
1/4 teaspoon nutmeg
Slivers of orange rind

In a blender or food processor, combine the dates and juices. Blend until the dates are finely chopped. Add the bananas along with the yogurt and nutmeg, blending until smooth. Pour into an 8-inch metal pan or bowl. Freeze until firm.

Remove from the freezer and beat vigorously with a whisk or electric beater until creamy but not melted. Cover and freeze until firm. Remove from freezer 15 minutes before serving to soften. Beat again for a smoother consistency.

Garnish with slivers of orange rind on each serving.

Yield: 3 cups

Orange Sherbet

This simple sherbet can be spectacular when it is served in the scooped out halves of oranges or lemons.

1-1/2 cups low-fat milk
2 tablespoons nonfat dry
   milk powder
3/4 cup frozen orange juice
   concentrate, at room
   temperature
2 tablespoons frozen apple
   juice concentrate, at room
   temperature
1 tablespoon grated orange
   rind
1 egg white, at room
   temperature
1 orange, peeled, segmented,
   and cut into chunks

Combine the milk and dry milk powder, beating until well-combined. Mix in the orange and apple juice concentrates and orange rind.

Beat the egg white until stiff but not dry. Fold into the orange mixture. Pour into an 8-inch metal pan or bowl, and freeze until the sherbet is solid around the edge and the center is still mushy. Remove from the freezer and beat vigorously with a whisk or electric beater until creamy but not melted. Cover and freeze until firm. Remove from the freezer 15 minutes before serving to soften. Beat again for a smoother consistency.

Garnish individual servings with orange chunks.

Yield: 3 cups

Fruit Sauces & Toppings

In this chapter is a collection of fruit sauces, spreads, and toppings to finish off your desserts.

The vibrantly flavorful fruit sauces are delicious blends of fresh fruit and fruit juice sweeteners. Fruit juice enhances the taste of the fruit, whereas sugar masks the flavor with a bland sweetness. We use the sauces as toppings for ice cream, crêpes, and puddings, as well as cakes. The fruit spreads and jams are, of course, wonderful on toast. But we include them here because they are also wonderful as a low-calorie alternative to pastry creams and whipped cream. We use fruit spreads instead of pastry cream to line tarts and we use them as toppings for cakes and puddings. Store fruit spreads in the refrigerator for up to 3 weeks or freeze them in small containers, leaving an inch at the top to allow for expansion.

Finally, we have a variety of whipped toppings made with low-fat milk, low-fat evaporated milk, low-fat cottage cheese, and so on. These toppings make terrific low-calorie substitutes for whipped cream.

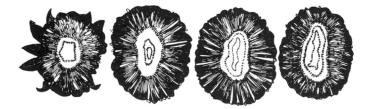

Fruit Sauces and Toppings   201

Spicy Apple Butter

To capture the flavor and fragrance of the fall apple crop, invest some time in early autumn in making apple butter. It takes about 45 minutes to prepare and will keep for many weeks in the refrigerator or longer if frozen. The recipe can be successfully doubled in quantity.

8 medium-size apples
  (about 2 pounds), peeled
  (optional), cored, and
  sliced into sixths
1/2 cup frozen apple juice
  concentrate
1/2 cup water
2 teaspoons cinnamon
3/4 teaspoon allspice

In a heavy-bottomed deep saucepan, combine the apples, apple juice concentrate, and water. Simmer, covered, for 20 minutes. Remove from the heat and puree in a blender, food processor, or food mill with the cinnamon and allspice. Return the pureed mixture to the saucepan and cook over low heat until it becomes a thick paste, 45 to 60 plus minutes, depending on the variety of apple. It is important to stir the puree frequently to prevent scorching. Partially cover the pan to contain hot splatters, while still letting the steam evaporate.

Store the apple butter in covered containers in the refrigerator. It also freezes well.

Yield: Scant 4 cups

Pear Butter. Substitute 8 medium-size pears for the apples. Add 2 teaspoons grated lemon rind and 1 table-spoon lemon juice.

Strawberry Jam

Nothing can equal homemade jam on toast. Double the quantities if you wish.

2 cups fresh sliced
   strawberries (or 12 ounces
   unsweetened frozen and
   defrosted strawberries)
1/3 cup frozen apple juice
   concentrate
1/4 cup water
1/2 cup finely chopped
   dried apple slices

In a small saucepan, heat the strawberries, apple juice concentrate, water, and dried apple. Simmer, uncovered, over low heat, stirring frequently for 10 to 15 minutes, or until the fruits are soft and all the liquid is absorbed. Refrigerate in tightly covered jars for several weeks or freeze.

Yield: 2 cups

Cherry Jam. Substitute pitted and halved cherries, fresh or frozen and defrosted, for the strawberries and proceed as directed above.

Apricot Jam

1 cup chopped dried apricots
Equal parts frozen apple
   juice concentrate and water

Soak the apricots overnight in just enough apple juice concentrate and water to cover. Simmer, uncovered, in a saucepan over low heat, stirring frequently until the apricots are very soft and all the liquid is absorbed. If the apricots are very tart, add 1 to 2 tablespoons more apple juice concentrate and cook until absorbed. Strain or puree. Refrigerate in tightly covered jars for several weeks or freeze.

Yield: 1 cup

Pineapple-Apricot Marmalade

Spoon this confection over yogurt or serve it with warm muffins.

1-1/3 cups dried apricots
1 (20-ounce) can
  unsweetened crushed
  pineapple with juice
Additional unsweetened
  fruit juices (pineapple,
  apple, or orange)
1/4 cup frozen apple juice
  concentrate
2 teaspoons grated orange
  rind

Place the apricots in a small saucepan. Drain the juice from the pineapple into a large measuring cup. Set the pineapple aside. Add additional fruit juice so that the liquid measures 1-3/4 cups. Pour over the apricots. Bring just to a boil, reduce the heat, and simmer for 20 minutes or until tender.

Puree the apricot mixture in a blender or food processor with the apple juice concentrate. Return the mixture to the saucepan and stir in the crushed pineapple and orange rind. Cook over low heat, stirring constantly, for about 5 minutes, or until the mixture is heated through and all the liquid is absorbed. When cool, refrigerate in tightly covered jars.

Yield: 3 to 3-1/2 cups

Strawberry Sauce

This ruby-red sauce can dress up rice pudding or beautify a melon wedge or a bowl of sliced peaches.

2 cups fresh strawberries
  (or 12 ounces unsweetened
  frozen and defrosted
  strawberries)
2 tablespoons frozen apple
  juice concentrate
3 tablespoons orange juice

Slice the berries. Set aside 1/2 cup.

In a small saucepan, combine the remaining 1-1/2 cups berries with the apple juice concentrate and orange juice. Bring to a boil, then reduce the heat, and simmer gently until the berries are very soft, about 5 minutes. Press the berries through a fine sieve and discard the pulp. Cool. Stir in the remaining 1/2 cup berries. Serve chilled.

Yield: 2-1/4 cups

Black Cherry Sauce

Deep purplish-red, whole cherries make up this sauce. It is very much at home over crêpes, cakes, fruits, and ices or swirled through yogurt.

2 cups pitted black cherries (fresh, canned, or unsweetened frozen and defrosted)
1/4 cup frozen apple juice concentrate
Grape juice as needed
1 tablespoon cornstarch
3 tablespoons grape juice
2 teaspoons grated orange rind (optional)

Drain and reserve any cherry juices. Combine the apple juice concentrate and cherry juice with enough grape juice to make 3/4 cup. Place the cherries and liquid in a small saucepan. Boil for 1 minute. Dissolve the cornstarch in the 3 tablespoons grape juice and add with the orange rind. Boil for 1 minute, stirring constantly until thickened. Serve immediately or transfer to a bowl and cover the surface with plastic wrap to prevent a skin from forming. Refrigerate until needed.

Yield: 2-1/2 cups

Melba Sauce

Made with either strawberries or raspberries, this sauce has a beautiful rosy color. Serve it over cake, peach halves, or other fruit.

2 cups sliced fresh strawberries or raspberries (or 12 ounces unsweetened frozen and defrosted berries)
1/4 cup frozen apple juice concentrate
1/4 cup orange juice
2 teaspoons grated orange rind
2 teaspoons cornstarch
2 tablespoons orange juice
1 teaspoon brandy extract (optional)

Place the berries in a small saucepan with the apple juice concentrate, 1/4 cup orange juice, and orange rind. Bring to a boil, reduce the heat, and simmer for 5 minutes or until the berries are very soft. Press through a sieve, discarding the pulp. Return the strained juice to the saucepan. Bring to a boil. Dissolve the cornstarch in the remaining 2 tablespoons orange juice and add to the saucepan. Boil for 1 minute, stirring constantly until the sauce is thick and clear. Stir in the brandy extract. Transfer to a bowl. Cover the surface with plastic wrap to prevent a skin from forming and refrigerate. Serve chilled.

Yield: 1-1/2 cups

Orange Sauce

This lively citrus sauce can be used over crêpes, cake, or puddings. Consider adding fresh chunks of orange or tangerine to the sauce just before serving.

2 tablespoons cornstarch
1/4 cup frozen apple juice
   concentrate, at room
   temperature
3 tablespoons frozen orange
   juice concentrate, at room
   temperature
1 teaspoon grated orange rind
1-1/2 cups low-fat milk
1 egg yolk, slightly beaten

Combine the cornstarch, juice concentrates, and orange rind in a small saucepan. Gradually stir in the milk. Cook over low heat, stirring constantly, until the mixture just begins to thicken. Remove from the heat. Stir 2 teaspoons of the sauce into the beaten egg yolk. Return the saucepan to the heat and stir the egg yolk into the cornstarch mixture. Cook, stirring constantly, until the mixture just comes to a boil and thickens. Remove from the heat. Serve immediately or cover the surface with plastic wrap to prevent a skin from forming and refrigerate until needed.

Yield: 2 cups

Glazed Diced Orange Peel

With its irresistible zesty taste, these glistening bits of orange peels are as tempting as candy. Use glazed peel or strips to dramatize and decorate simple desserts.

2 thick-skinned oranges
6 tablespoons frozen apple
   juice concentrate

Remove the orange peel, including the white pith, and cut into 1/4-inch cubes. Reserve the orange pulp and juice for another use.

To remove the bitterness, place the cubes in a small saucepan with water to cover. Bring to a boil. Simmer for 5 minutes. Drain. Repeat the process once more, then rinse, drain, and pat dry with a towel.

Place the peel in a heavy-bottomed saucepan with the apple juice concentrate and simmer until all the liquid is absorbed and the peel is glazed. Use in cookies, cakes, breads, and puddings and as a garnish.

Yield: Approximately 1 cup

Glazed Orange Peel Strips

2 oranges
3 tablespoons frozen apple
  juice concentrate

With a vegetable peeler, remove just the orange part of the rind of the 2 oranges. Cut into very fine strips.

Place the strips in a small saucepan, cover with water, and boil for 5 minutes. Drain. Repeat the process. Rinse the strips, drain, and pat dry.

Place the strips in a heavy-bottomed saucepan with the apple juice concentrate and simmer until the liquid is absorbed and the strips are glazed. Use as a garnish for fruits, puddings, and cakes.

Yield: Approximately 1/2 cup

Glazed Ginger Root

Use these small bits of pungent ginger to flavor bread, cake, cookies, ice cream, and crêpes.

1/2 cup (about 2-1/2 ounces)
  peeled and thinly sliced
  fresh ginger root
1/2 cup frozen apple juice
  concentrate

To mellow the strong ginger flavor, place the slices in a small saucepan with water to cover. Bring to a boil. Simmer for 5 minutes. Rinse and drain. Repeat this process 3 more times. Then rinse, drain, and dry the slices by patting with a towel. Place the slices in a small heavy saucepan with the apple juice concentrate and simmer, stirring frequently, until all the liquid is absorbed and the peel is glazed.

Store in a sealed container in the refrigerator for a few days or keep indefinitely in the freezer.

Yield: 1/2 cup

Orange Glaze

Use over light fruits such as pineapple, peaches, bananas, grapes, kiwi fruit.

3/4 cup orange juice
2 teaspoons cornstarch
1 teaspoon grated orange rind

In a small saucepan, combine 1 tablespoon of the orange juice with the cornstarch; stir until the cornstarch is dissolved. Add the remaining orange juice and orange rind. Bring slowly to a boil; boil for 1 minute, stirring constantly until thickened. Transfer to a bowl. Cover the surface with plastic wrap to prevent a skin from forming. Refrigerate until needed.

Yield: Approximately 3/4 cup

Strawberry Glaze

Use over dark fruits, such as cherries and berries.

1 cup crushed or sliced
   fresh strawberries (or
   unsweetened frozen and
   defrosted strawberries)
1/2 cup frozen apple juice
   concentrate
1/4 cup water
1-1/2 tablespoons cornstarch
2 tablespoons water

In a small saucepan, combine the strawberries with the apple juice concentrate and 1/4 cup water. Bring to a boil, reduce the heat, and simmer for 5 minutes. Rub through a sieve, discarding the pulp. Return the strained juice to the saucepan and bring to a boil once again. Dissolve the cornstarch in the remaining 2 tablespoons water. Add to the saucepan and boil for 1 minute, stirring constantly, until the sauce is thickened and clear. Transfer to a bowl. Cover the surface with plastic wrap to prevent a skin from forming. Refrigerate until needed.

Yield: 1-1/3 cups

Apricot Glaze

1 cup chopped dried apricots
Equal parts frozen apple
   juice concentrate and water
2 tablespoons frozen apple
   juice concentrate
2 tablespoons water

Soak the apricots overnight in just enough apple juice concentrate and water to cover. Simmer, uncovered, in a saucepan over low heat. Stir frequently until the apricots are very soft and all the liquid is absorbed. Strain or puree. Return the mixture to the saucepan and add the 2 tablespoons each of apple juice concentrate and water. Heat for 1 to 2 minutes or until the mixture is combined. Transfer to a bowl. Cover the surface with plastic wrap to prevent a skin from forming. Refrigerate until needed.

Yield: 1-1/3 cups

Light Milk Whip

This is a whipped milk version of whipped cream that cuts way back on calories and fat.

1/2 cup low-fat evaporated
  milk
1-1/2 tablespoons frozen
  apple juice concentrate
1/2 teaspoon lemon juice
1/2 teaspoon vanilla extract

Measure the milk into a mixer bowl and place in the freezer along with the beaters for the mixer. Chill until ice crystals form around the edge, 20 to 30 minutes.

Beat the milk with an electric mixer at its highest speed. When soft peaks form, add the apple juice concentrate, lemon juice, and vanilla. Continue to beat until fluffy.

Serve at once or keep in the refrigerator for 10 minutes. Light Milk Whip can be prepared ahead and kept for up to 2 days if it is stabilized with gelatin, see variation below.

Yield: 3 cups

Light Milk Whip II. Pour 1/4 cup unsweetened fruit juice into a heatproof cup or bowl and sprinkle 1 envelope of unflavored gelatin over it. Place the cup holding the gelatin mixture in a pan of simmering water and stir until the gelatin is dissolved. Combine with 3/4 cup unsweetened fruit juice. Chill, stirring occasionally, until the mixture is syrupy but not set. Prepare a recipe of Light Milk Whip. When fluffy, fold in the gelatin mixture. Serve immediately or refrigerate for up to 2 days.

Trim Topping

A low-fat topping that can be accented with spices or flavorings. It is very good over fresh fruits.

1 pint low-fat cottage cheese
1/4 cup plain nonfat yogurt
2 tablespoons frozen apple
   juice concentrate, at room
   temperature
Grated lemon or orange
   rind, cinnamon, nutmeg,
   vanilla extract, or brandy
   extract
Currants or nuts

Place the cottage cheese in a strainer and press out any excess liquid. Combine with the yogurt in a food processor or blender. Blend for several minutes, until smooth. Scrape down the sides of the bowl; add one of the flavorings and blend once again. Stir in the currants or nuts. Refrigerate for 1 hour before using.

Yield: 2-1/4 cups

Whipped Cheese Topping

This is a most pleasant topping to spread on dessert breads in general, and Fig Torte and Gingerbread in particular. Flavor it with bits of Glazed Ginger Root (page 207) or Glazed Orange Peel (page 206-207) and use it to fill dessert crêpes.

1 cup low-fat cottage cheese
2 tablespoons frozen apple
   juice concentrate, at room
   temperature
1 teaspoon grated lemon rind
1 teaspoon lemon juice
1 cup low-fat sour cream
1/4 teaspoon cinnamon

Place the cottage cheese in a strainer and squeeze out any excess liquid. In a food processor or blender, beat the cottage cheese with the apple juice concentrate, lemon rind, and lemon juice until well blended. Add the sour cream and cinnamon and beat until fluffy. Store covered in the refrigerator for several hours before using.

Yield: 2 cups

Cream Cheese Topping

This topping makes the traditional frosting to top off a carrot cake, but it also makes a fine spread for piping hot muffins.

8 ounces low-fat cream
  cheese, at room
  temperature
2 teaspoons grated lemon rind
2 tablespoons frozen apple
  juice concentrate
1/2 teaspoon vanilla extract

Mix the cream cheese, lemon rind, apple juice concentrate, and vanilla until smooth; then beat until fluffy. Refrigerate until you are ready to spread on a cake.

Yield: Frosting for two 8-inch cake layers or one 9-inch by 13-inch cake

Index